100
Legendary
Knives

Original title in French: *100 Couteaux de légende*
© 2000 Copyright Studio—Paris, France
© 2002 Krause Publications—Iola—USA
for the American edition

Published by

krause publications

700 East State Street • Iola, WI 54990-0001
715-445-2214 • www.krause.com

Please call or write for our free catalog. Our toll-free number to place an order or obtain a free catalog is 800-258-0929.

Library of Congress Catalog Number: 2001096278

ISBN: 0-87349-417-2

Printed in Spain

100
Legendary
Knives

TEXT AND PHOTOGRAPHS

GÉRARD PACELLA

kp krause publications
since 1952

700 East State Street • Iola, WI 54990-0001
715-445-2214 • www.krause.com

contents

The knife, a tool as old as the hills

"In the beginning…" Thus commences Genesis, the first book of the Bible. But it would perhaps not be all that blasphemous to rewrite that phrase as follows: "In the beginning was the knife, man's first tool." But without rewriting the history of the world, let's just say that our oldest ancestors, the pre-hominoids from eastern Africa, appeared around four million years ago. In the first Paleolithic period man evolved to standing upright, developed skills, discovered fire, and started hunting big game. He now had to skin animals to clothe himself and cut up meat to eat. To do all this he needed a tool, and this tool was flint, the first knife of humanity!

The technique for cutting flint consisted initially of striking one block against another block, to employ the expression generally used in scientific circles. Over the years this technique improved, with the flint being held in the hand and struck against a large rock serving as an anvil. Having got rid of the jagged shards on both sides, the flint was now almond-shaped. Hewing and cutting skills continued to advance and gestures became more precise, which led to ever finer edges. As for the shards, they were also used but were only worked on one side, the other side remaining smooth, as opposed to the larger flint which was worked on both sides.

With Neanderthal man appeared tools that were not only more sophisticated but had quite specific uses. Procedures evolved, with flints being fashioned using bone or wood hammers, enabling triangular points to be obtained. Scrapers were also made so as to clean skins better, and the idea of putting a flint at the end of a wooden shaft became commonplace, resulting in effective clubs for hunting.

The various periods of prehistory succeeded each other, bringing new techniques and materials: spearheads, ever finer and razor-sharp flint blades, and development of bone and ivory crafts. The simple flint tool held between thumb and forefinger became

*Prehistoric man?
Already an artist!*

*Facing page: cave paintings
are an invaluable legacy.*

*The perfection
of certain twin-
faced tools tells
us a lot about
our ancestors'
technological
know-how.*

Utilitarian objects for sure, but the need to personalize them, to make them beautiful, at the price of meticulous workmanship, already existed.

cate are the sculptures and so wonderfully carved are the knives.

But man was nomadic at this time, following the migrations of the animals that constituted his food supply or fleeing during the ice age, the regions that had become too cold. Continents were formed and the various tribes scattered, becoming civilizations that all evolved differently according to their geographical and climatic situation. But whatever the longitude or latitude in Africa, America, Asia, Europe or the Pacific, the knife remained man's faithful companion, used both as a tool and as a weapon. Intelligence developed, civilizations evolved, and one age succeeded another… Eventually, with the discovery of minerals and skillful mastery of fire, metallurgy was born.

a straight knife in itself, either hewn in one piece with blade on one side and shaft on the other, or else in two parts with a piece of wood, bone, horn or ivory for the shaft and a piece of hewn flint for the blade, the two halves joined using a ligature made of plant fibers or animal tendons. They even made glue by heating these very same animal tendons in order to liquefy them!

But primitive as he was, man had already started to decorate his environment and embellish his possessions, as can be seen from the rock paintings, sculpture and pottery that have survived to this day. The same aesthetic care was also lavished on his hunting weapons, on bows, spears, and of course knives. One only has to travel to the Périgord, or visit certain museums in other regions, to realize the beauty of these objects, true works of art, so deli-

Copper came first, but since this metal did not possess the required qualities to replace stone, tin was added to it, which produced bronze. But this alloy was not easy to master, which is why this relatively long period, called the Bronze Age, is generally divided into three parts: the Early Bronze Age, the Middle Bronze Age, and the Late Bronze Age. The kinds of knives produced during this long period are quite astounding; the modernism of the design of some of them leaves one agape at how advanced the techniques were at the time given the lack of materials and perfected tools.

With the passing of prehistory came the Iron Age, which opened the doors to the modern era. Ironwork created infinite possibilities, not only for knives, but for metallurgy in general, a decisive step for humanity. The centuries rolled by, from the first to the 21st, during which time objects and crafts appeared and disappeared. But knives and their makers (cutlers) have endured the ages, despite periods of recession, gradually organizing and consolidating their trade, creating centers of excellence to ensure the continued manufacture of quality blades, both in times of peace and of war, whether for use in the home, at work or for combat.

We still don't know if the "willow-leaf" shape was intended for a specific use or if it was a stylistic piece, a "craft" object of its time.

A man with a knife at his belt in full view clearly shows his status, as well as enabling him to face attack, since the desire to forcefully seize or threaten another person's goods or valuables is as old as time itself. It should not be forgotten that the table knife, like the fork, appeared relatively late, around the 15th century. You simply used the knife you carried with you. The Gauls, for example, all carried a short straight knife in a leather sheath. As for the folding, or clasp knife, it is mentioned by historians as far back as the 5th century BC. During the Gallo-Roman period, the principle of a blade swiveling on an axis to fold into the handle was already known. However, it was not until the 18th century that it came into general use, a delay that can be explained by several reasons.

The first reason is technical. It was not easy to discover and perfect the spring mechanism that would block the blade in both the open and closed positions, since "modern" tools were required to achieve sufficient reliability of operation. The second reason concerns customs and behavior. For many a long century, it was essential to clearly display one's power, that is to say one's strength of wealth. A sturdy weapon would thus provoke fear, while a richly decorated one would oblige respect. Either way, this external sign enabled one either to know who one was dealing with, or else attempt to pass oneself off for something one was not... It is clear that a folding knife buried deep in one's pocket did not provide any such prestige.

The knife has survived the ages as man's faithful companion, from Cro-Magnon to astronaut. Today, the knife is an effective tool, an amusing object, a fearsome weapon or the canvas for a work of art. The cutler of the third millennium performs exactly the same gestures in the exercise of his craft as his predecessors of centuries past, just as the hunter skins and carves up the same game as Australopithecus did. The knife is indeed the incontestable link between eras and civilizations; to examine its history is to examine the history of mankind.

Certain bows, despite their functional nature, were beautifully carved, as one can see here.

Below: Blade grinders of Thiers.

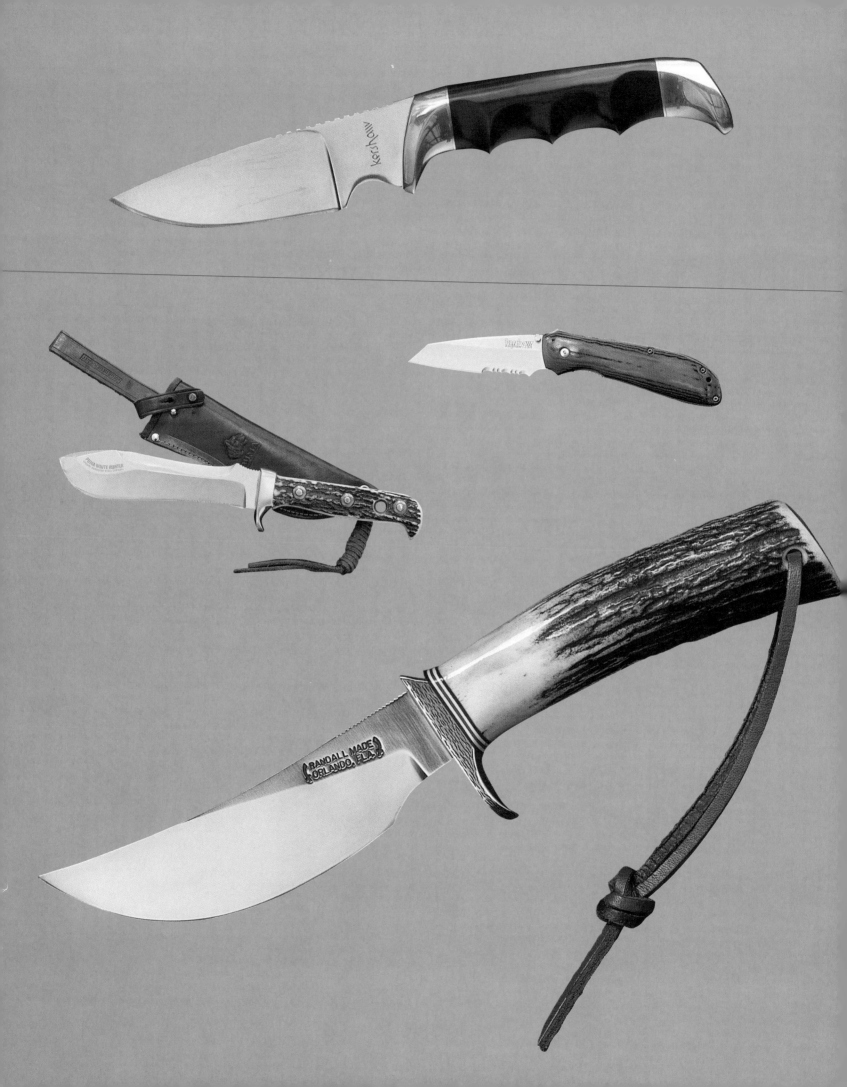

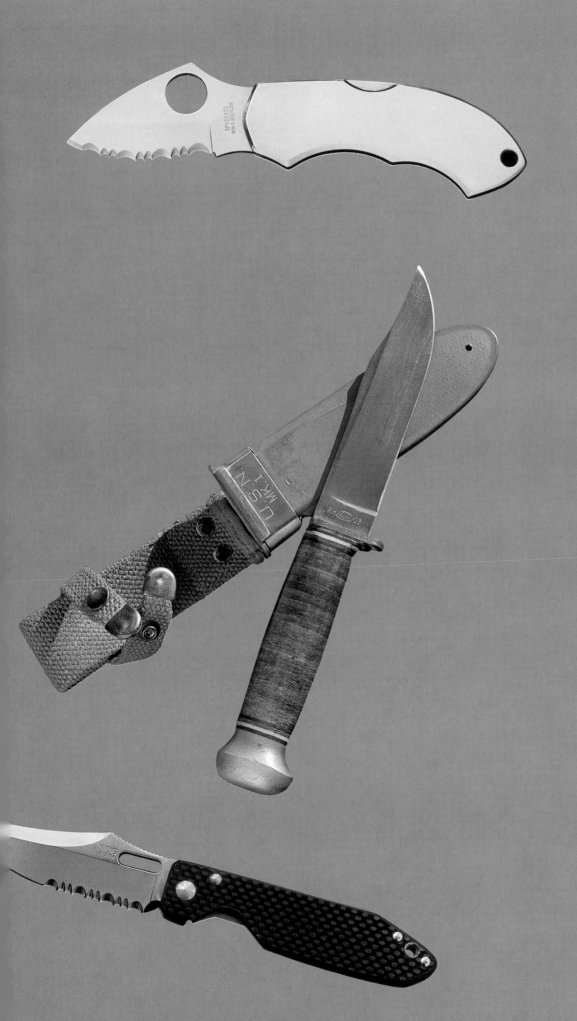

Powder damascene

A powerful damascene blade with its subtle nuances.

W hen he started producing his first knives for sale in 1970, Wolf Borger naturally chose for his logo a wolf howling at the moon.

This young German, one of the few full-time knife craftsmen in his country, is fired by many passions: hunting, fishing, canoeing, music. A ceaseless traveler, he speaks several languages fluently and has studied both modern American and Native American history.

Wolf Borger.

He qualified as a Master Cutler in 1986 and works comfortably in all styles.

Like his fellow countryman, Dietmar Kressler, he has a keen interest in metallurgy, keeps abreast of the latest developments in steel production, and insists on handling the tempering of his knives personally, so as to be sure of the result.

In August 1995, he was present at the opening of Damasteel in Sweden, where he discovered "powder damascene," which he immediately started to use and helped to make known all over the world. This new steel, RWL 34, has unsurpassable advantages due to its high carbide-composition, forming a very fine and particularly regular structure, which provides greater solidity for less thickness, with a durable cutting edge. He even learned the steel-

smith's craft so as to improve the qualities of this astounding alloy, succeeding in obtaining PMC 27! The design and shape of the waves are truly beautiful in an entirely different way to traditional damascene.

For a long time the straight knife was his area of predilection, but he has never been a man to get stuck in his ways, which is why he recently turned his skills to folding knives.

A man who respects tradition, when he attends the Munich Knife Fair each year, he never fails to display a few of his "nickers," those typically German knives, but with that special Wolf Borger touch, a blade of powder damascene.

Wolf Borger's production also includes high-tech knives.

Dietmar Kressler.

The leader of
the German cutlery industry

Useful, but also beautiful.

I n Germany, nature is vast. An essential accessory for hunting, fishing, hiking or camping, a knife is also indispensable for all those who work in the countryside. The cutlery tradition is thus of much greater importance there than in France, but it is interesting to note that while Frenchmen like Jean Tanazacq and Henri Viallon have many imitators, the same is not at all true for Germany.

Dietmar Kressler left his native Bavaria to join the army. In 1971, at twenty-five years old, he was posted to the United States where he sold the knife that he had made himself, as is the custom in his country.

During a trip while on leave he visited a knife show where he met the already famous craftsman A. J. Russel. They got along very well, and Russel agreed to train him.

Since the pupil was a fast learner and showed himself to be particularly gifted, Russel recommended him to the greatest crafts-

man of the time, Bob Loveless. Kressler spent all of his spare time in this sorcerer's cave, where he learned all of the subtleties of the craft and met all of the top people in the profession. In 1974, Sergeant Kressler returned to Germany, enriched by a sturdy cutlery apprenticeship. He hung up his uniform five years later, but not without having first set up a workshop and perfected a whole range of straight knives in the purest American style.

In 1981, after having acquired a set of high-performance tools, he turned professional full time, becoming one of the few cutlery craftsmen to exercise their profession in complete exclusivity. Things haven't changed much since then in Europe. At present there are only five of them.

A Kressler knife is clearly characteristic of its maker, who is unanimously appreciated and recognized in Europe, Japan and the United States as a highly talented knifemaker.

The best from the young Bavarian; making a knife like this is a delicate operation.

The precursor
of an evolving profession

Jean Tanazacq.

France is undoubtedly a country with a strong cutlery tradition. Over the centuries numerous knife-making towns have played their role: Paris, Nogent, Rouen, Châtellerault, Toulouse, and so many others. But even though all manufacture was by hand, particularly before modern automation, knives were still made on production lines, with each worker responsible for a specific task. This meant that there were few cutlers capable of producing all parts for a knife themselves; their work consisted more of assembling those produced in series by other workers. In the United States, for example, the tradition, indeed principle, of complete manufacture by a craftsman is still very much alive (despite the large number of manufacturers that have sprung up since the end of the 19th century) to such an extent that knowledge and technique have been handed down from generation to generation. So while production-line knives continued to leave Nogent and Thiers and with not a single cutler craftsman in the whole of France, one man decided to throw himself into an unbelievable

adventure. Jean Tanazacq was born in 1939 in the Ardennes, and in 1959 commenced his studies at the National Institute of Applied Sciences in Lyon, leaving four years later with an engineer's diploma in his pocket. After completing his military service as an officer, he spent a number of years with Citroën, during which time he familiarized himself with their manufacturing and metalworking methods, followed by a few years with the National Scientific Research Center to give him a quite considerable experience. His passion for knives started as a child, perhaps influenced by his grandfather, who had experienced the Franco-Prussian War of 1870, the Great War of 1914-1918, and the Second World War. Then, of course, there was his upbringing in the Ardennes, where there was a hardly a family that didn't hunt wild boar. Alongside his studies and various professional activities, he undertook detailed research of knife manufacture. This was not an easy task, since it was difficult to find books and documents on the subject, and he was all on his own. But he persevered and, in 1977, felt

"Prairie" dagger; available in various lengths.

The first in the long "Tronçay" range.

himself ready to give up the comfort of a steady and well-paid job to launch himself into a profession that he had to build almost from scratch.

By 1980, he had not only found premises, finance and materials, but produced a catalog presenting a particularly wide range. The adventure had begun! Tanazacq decided to leave folding knives and concentrate on straight models. The first range was intended essentially for hunters, and he immediately had unbelievable success with them, astonishing many people, not least being the designer himself. Up until then, hunters had been used to mass-produced knives bought at relatively low prices, and having nothing in common with 100 percent handmade ones.

Jean Tanazacq succeeded in solving the equation of stainless-steel quality/cutting-power/resistance to snapping by shock or bending. This was not a simple task, since the greater the cutting power required the less resistant the steel is, except if it is carbon-based, in which case it oxidizes. So he chose the method involving the cutting of steel bars, rather than the forging method. The first users were hooked, rumor spread, and his success was assured. Each model bears an evocative name like the "Tronçay" range, for example, or the "Prairie," "Rix," "Charleville," "Rocroy," and "Ventoux" ranges, as well as single models made to order.

The military, always on the lookout for the best blades, soon came knocking at the door of this inventive Ardennes guy, requesting special models or else identical reproductions of certain American combat knives. Even the Fire Service called round and got him to make them a special diving knife. With their incomparable mirror polish, the continuity of Tanazacq blades is assured by his son, Nicolas!

A sturdy blade, suitable for any use…

Rekindling the forge

Henri Viallon.

An infinite range of straight models made to this design.

There is nothing original about being born in Thiers to a family that has been producing knives for four generations and wanting to continue the same profession. However, the career of the man who rekindled the forges of his town, perhaps even his country, merits the detour. Thiers, the capital of French cutlery, is testimony to five centuries of activity, during which time each workshop was given responsibility for a specific stage in the production line. But despite a solid experience gleaned since 1975 in various workshops involved in the manufacture of folding knives, the essentials remained to be learned. It was only when he arrived at the Maison des Couteliers that young Henri Viallon was able to learn the steps hitherto unknown to him, taught by the only truly

"Celestial storm." View of the earth "setting," as seen from the moon, in which Henri Viallon shows all his skill: damascene, different alloys, inlaying, etc.

accomplished craftsmen of the moment: Munnoz, Angel Navarro, and De Nardi. In 1984, he made a decisive discovery in the cellar… an old forge that he rushed to restore and get working.

Impassioned, he heard of damascene that the American cutlers had brought back into fashion. It was in books like *The Cutler's Art,* written in old French by Jean-Jacques Perret in 1771, as well the monumental work of Camille Page, rare documentation that Cutlery Museum was very lucky to have in its possession, that he discovered the rudiments of this craft. He spent all of his spare time scouring neighboring farms for old iron and grinders. But the absence of a master was clearly felt, and progress was extremely slow… He discovered borax from a French Canadian he met in the town, finally came to master binding, and armed with his trusty hammer eventually produced his first damascene—fifty-six layers! Taking his inspiration from the photographs of American knives that had started to appear in magazines, he created a line that eventually led him to set up as a cutler in 1987.

He has been ceaselessly producing his knives ever since, even going so far as to resuscitate certain long-forgotten traditional regional models. A pioneer of long lineage, France owes the rekindling of her forges to his perseverance and craft.

The Dutchman who dreamed of America

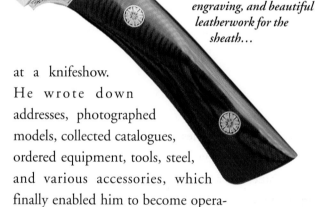

Perfect finishing, discreet engraving, and beautiful leatherwork for the sheath…

I n Holland there has always been a plethora of cheeses, but never any beautiful knives to cut them with.

This is perhaps what Frans van den Heuvel thought when, with his own hands, he produced the first knife in a long line that he certainly couldn't have dreamed of at the time.

His technical studies led him to specialize in the production of machine-tools, but as a hunter and shooter, he had always loved knives, even producing them in his spare time for his personal use, and then for his close friends. But he lacked technique, the relevant documentation, and didn't know what kind of tools he should use. So someone gave him an address in the United States, that of Corbet Sigman, one of the oldest cutlers who, like the majority of the American professionals, immediately supplied him generously with what he requested, and more.

He thus learned from across the water, before coming Stateside where he was finally able to meet his teacher in person, as well as the great bladesmiths,

Frans van den Heuvel.

at a knifeshow.

He wrote down addresses, photographed models, collected catalogues, ordered equipment, tools, steel, and various accessories, which finally enabled him to become operational. In 1980, now aged forty-three, Frans van den Heuvel founded Hill Knives and immediately started producing top quality blades. His first customer was the well known Swiss cutler Jean-Pierre Klöszli, who encouraged him to do even better. Each model received a personalized engraving, the sheath was made from the most beautiful skins and all kinds of knives were foreseen for all uses, eventualities and according to the style of the moment.

A proof of continuity, as well as fresh blood, his son Albert now assists his father.

Precious, but sober…

17

The first legendary smith

Is this what James Black's knives looked like?

I f Vulcan, the Roman god of Fire and Metalworking, ever decided to make a trip down to earth, he would certainly have done so on the 1st of May 1800, in New Jersey.

At any rate, that was where a certain James Black, considered to be the first legendary American knife-smith, was born. After ten years training in a workshop producing silver objects, the young James was attracted by the forge and got himself hired as an apprentice by a certain Shaw, in Arkansas, whose daughter he married. As the location, symbolically called the "frontier," was particularly strategic for business, Black decided to stay there and succeed his father-in-law.

The blades he forged were excellent and using his silversmith experience, he decorated the handles with the most beautiful inlays. This mix of beauty, quality and functionality earned his knives a superb reputation, with people coming from far away to place their orders. Not only did he attach great importance to finding the best shapes and sizes for given tasks, as well as fitting the customer's hand, but he labored endlessly to perfect the quality of the metal.

We can indeed say that he had understood everything about this mysterious alchemy, that of sublimating the qualities of a steel through fire and hammer, since we know that he even discovered the secret of damascene in his smithy.

He made tests with all the alloys he could get his hands on, and preciously hoarded a meteorite he found during a walk, intending to make use of it for an exceptional occasion. The opportunity came in 1830 when the reputation of this devilish bladesmith reached the ears of Jim Bowie. So it was not by chance that James Black, considered to be the precursor and model of American master bladesmiths, became a legend.

You can imagine James Black striking his anvil for hours on end…

Metalsmiths have always been fascinated by meteorites.

Scagel produced an unimaginable number of knives.

The clear reference

No photograph exists of Old Bill, just this charcoal portrait made a long time ago…

Although James Black certainly existed, as is clearly proven by the numerous articles published at the time concerning him, there exists not a trace, not a vestige of a single one of the numerous knives he produced; indeed the only descriptions we have come from those very same press cuttings. Fortunately, the situation is completely different for Bill Scagel, the second legendary bladesmith. "Old Bill," as he was usually called, was born in Ontario in 1873. After an unhappy marriage, he decided to turn his back definitively on civilization to go and live as a true hermit in a trapper's cabin with only beavers and raccoons for company.

From 1930 onwards, he commenced a passion for huge black Labradors, which were perfect for retrieving the wild ducks he regularly hunted from the icy water. Faced with a tough forest life and the various requirements of fishing and hunting, he started to make his own knives, basic perhaps, but each detail of them thought out according to a precise use. There is nothing but the essential in a Scagel knife: perfect size, balance, weight, proportions, with sober but sturdy materials. Each one had a detail that made it unique, proof that even in the wild forest, beauty and aesthetics were not neglected: here an inlay in copper or brass, there a strip of red leather to stand out, or the most beautiful part of a stag's antler for a pommel… The number of different models that this man was able forge with his own hands, without any assistance until his departure for another territory at ninety years old, is impressive: all shapes, types and sizes, without counting the saws and hatchets.

The whole range was an inspiration to modern American bladesmiths, starting with the man who bumped into him by chance one fine afternoon of 1937 on the shores of Lake Michigan, Bo Randall, who has almost all of Old Bill's models in his museum!

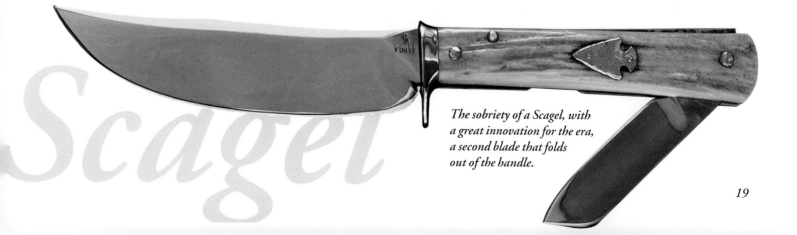

The sobriety of a Scagel, with a great innovation for the era, a second blade that folds out of the handle.

The living legend

If there is one bladesmith who has caused much ink to flow in every language, then it is certainly Bo Randall, already a legend in his lifetime. Nothing predestined this young man, working on his parents citrus plantation in Florida, to the art of cutlery, but life has many strange twists, turns and rare encounters, after which you are never the same again. A keen angler, Randall often traveled to the fish-filled waters of Lake Michigan with a knife slipped in his belt as it should be, this accessory that is so much a part of life in the United States for those who live close to nature. One day he spotted a man busy scraping the paint on his boat with a knife whose shape didn't fail to intrigue young Randall, so original was it: the knife was a Scagel, no more, no less!

The precious object changed hands (history does not say how), it was taken back to Florida, examined in detail, and an identical copy made on the plantation's forge. Randall, eager to meet this genius bladesmith

again, returned to Michigan and was able to gain access to the hermit's workshop. A solid friendship was born from this meeting, as well as a new vocation, but the move from plantation to forge was not instantaneous.

The first models were forged by Randall himself and could only be inspired by, even copied directly from, those of Scagel. However, since his lack of knowledge did not allow him to get past the stage of a simple hobbyist, he plowed through technical literature to try and fill in the various gaps before calling on the services of an experienced smith, which enabled him to stop manufacturing himself and concentrate on perfecting a range of models intended for anglers, hunters and trappers. The magnificent first catalog saw the light of day and, astoundingly enough, the most recent one, printed for the company's sixtieth birthday, is not only rigorously

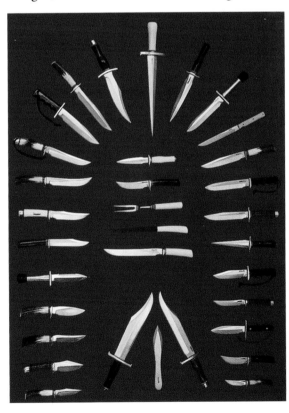

*A range just as vast
as that proposed by Scagel.*

*Forging a long blade is always
a delicate business, but Randall
made it his specialty.*

*One of
the first models
and still available today.*

identical as regards its layout, but still proposes models that were in the first one! Everything is continuity for this great company, including the manufacturing process, which is rather unconventional, since the cutler does not work on his own; the knives that leave the workshop being produced by a team. However, Randall always oversaw everything, designing the models and taking care of public relations with singular talent.

Apart from the vast "Outdoor" range, it has been the combat knives that have also helped to make the brand particularly famous. During World War II, many officers and members of special units carried a "Randall n°1," among them a certain Air Force captain that history boosted to the top rung in the country a few decades later: Ronald Reagan!

It was clear when the Vietnam War started that active units could not hope for anything better than a Randall, and a few models were perfected specially for them.

When the United States decided to undertake a new combat, that of space, a sturdy and reliable knife was an essential part of the astronauts' equipment, not for intergalactic combat, but survival in the event of a forced landing in an inhospitable area, like the jungle, instead of the base: once more it was to the Randall workshop that NASA turned!

The founder passed away to join Bill Scagel in 1989, but the brand continues, under the watchful eye of Gary, his son; now that's continuity!

Renewal with the forge and damascene

Scagel loved this kind of handle, but Moran has added all his sensitivity to it.

MORAN

The heritage that James Black and Bill Scagel left to American bladesmiths has been continued by Bill Moran. This man, whose generosity and talent are legendary, is a national living treasure. Now over seventy-five years old, this forge wizard has always lived in Maryland, working, learning and discovering on his own. After such a long working life (he started in 1942) one can only imagine how many times his hammer has struck his anvil.

Relearning the strokes and techniques of his two illustrious predecessors, he privileges the essential. The shapes of his knives are rather sober, but he forges blades of an incomparable quality. James Black liked to work silver inlays into the handles of his knives, and Bill Moran has continued this style, imagining the most beautiful scrolling. Bill Scagel, who loved the stars, sometimes placed a silver crescent moon, sun or stars on the handle or leather sheath, another idea that has also been continued by Moran.

Not only the very best steel, but also meteorites, have had occasion to pass through the fires of his forge, and even damascene, which he rediscovered. His first damascene knife dates from 1972, an event that shook the world of cutlery! But although he has always worked alone, he has never lived as a hermit; on the contrary he has generously shared his knowledge with everyone, going as far as to found the American Bladesmith Society, whose charter he wrote and whose chairman he was. With a view to educating the younger generation, he set up a metalsmith school that receives students all year round. In homage to his illustrious predecessor, he insisted that the premises be built on the very site where James Black had his forge.

With the talent of a genius and creator of a style admired by all professionals, Bill Moran is an artist in his own right!

A style that is pure Moran, pictured above.

Pure and original lines, perfectly mounted, with well-designed sheaths.

The Hollywood bladesmith

Powerful and indestructible; that's a Cooper for you!

I n September 1987, a great American bladesmith departed this earth at the age of eighty-one after a long and rich career. A short man, he spent his life making knives in a quite characteristic style that exercises great influence today on the creations of numerous craftsmen. Not only was he capable of producing all styles, but he also proposed a wide choice of options with no less than six styles of pommel and seven types of guard. Those who got to know him well, like Paul Basch, one of his few retailers, affirm that he created more than two hundred completely different models, not counting all those that differed by tiny details.

When the famous Bianchi brand, specializing in leather belts and holsters, decided to launch a range of knives whose sheaths would be produced in their own workshops, they turned to John Nelson Cooper, which says a lot about the renown of this man.

Movie studios had produced many films in which actors used knives, but they were always cheap props made from wood, whether Tarzan, war films or Westerns. But when Technicolor became standard for all adventure films, everything had to be much more realistic. Joseph Pevney, who made *Night of the Grizzly,* searched for the best bladesmith so that his hero, played by Clint Walker, would slip the most beautiful knife possible into his sheath. Cooper was asked to supply the superlative knife, and so entered into movie legend.

No Western was now complete without the main character's knife being a Cooper. Of note are *The Trackers,* with Sammy Davis Jr., and *The Iron Mistress,* with Alan Ladd, which is a rather florid, though historically inaccurate, account of the life of Jim Bowie, the famed bladesmith of the Old West, who we'll come across later.

John Nelson Cooper was a pioneer who blazed a trail that was soon followed by many others.

John Nelson Cooper.

The inventor
with a thousand talents

Before Bob Loveless, a straight knife consisted of a blade on one side, a handle on the other, and a guard in the middle, the whole ensemble carried in a leather sheath. However well made it was, it was just a functional object, what some would call a tool. The materials were traditional, with the shapes varying according to the use for which it was intended, but there had been nothing new under the sun for many a long decade.

With Loveless, the humble knife was suddenly raised to the rank of a work of art, and its standing soared, heralding a new era. How on earth did this man, still working today, go about revolutionizing a field that was an integral, almost institutionalized part of American culture?

A very active bladesmith, Loveless cut blades according to the orders he received. His production, of the highest quality, was not really any different from what other craftsmen were offering. The first idea he had was to develop a vast catalog that would include all types of knife. His second idea consisted of proposing sheaths that were not manufactured in advance, but designed according to the morphology and habits of the user, so that the handle would be immediately within reach.

A collector of pens, he had learned what made the difference between standard quality and truly beautiful manufacture. So he turned toward highly quality finishing, down to the tiniest details, setting prices that no longer bore any relation to those of his competitors. But to get himself known he also needed an individual style and unusual materials. He thus fathered new forms, including the "drop point" and the "semi-skinner," which were soon copied, as one might have expected…

Loveless also introduced surgical steels for the blades—154 CM and 440 C—as well as a previously unknown material for the handles, micarta, originally intended for the aeronautical industry. These steels are very hard and particularly tricky to grind, but the cutting edge is long-lasting. In addition, such hardness enables very fine grinding, as well as a mirror polish previously impossible to obtain. As for micarta, it is robust, rot-proof, waterproof, and available in different colors, as well as varying fineness of grain, enabling superb shimmer effects. Loveless produced relatively few, proposed special numbered series and got himself known all over the world, where his creations are vigorously sought after for high prices! He even went as far as perfecting different logos to add a touch of spice and entice collectors.

*Clean lines and
an alluring logo…*

Bob Loveless.

*A "handy" shape, always using
micarta for the handle.*

Before Loveless, the profession was in no way structured, with cutlers displaying their creations at arms shows. Loveless breathed a dynamism into the trade, resulting in the craftsmen forming their own guild, which enabled a charter to be drawn up and shows to be organized that focused exclusively on handmade knives. These shows were a godsend, not only for collectors, but also for the bladesmiths themselves who, apart from being able to get to know their clientele, were able to see what their fellows were doing, get advice and exchange ideas.

That is how our man with the colorful cap was immediately copied, in both form and material, but it is he who has become a legend, and he is irreplaceable…

Yes, Bob Loveless certainly ushered in a new era for American handmade knives!

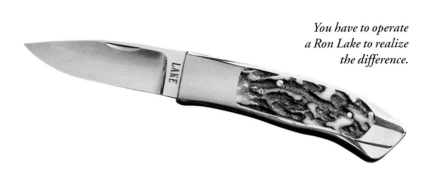

The "interframe" style

An interframe handle with the release-lever at the back: pure Ron Lake.

The Loveless method having proven its worth for the straight knife, there only remained to adapt it to the folding knife.

Bordered by Lake Michigan, Illinois is that state where nature runs free. Opportunities for hunting, fishing and hiking are not in short supply, although each inhabitant jealously guards his territory. Young Ron Lake started out by using knives from the major brands that were easy to get hold of in the shops, but very soon he began disassembling them to find out how the mechanisms worked; he would then adjust them before reassembling them. These improvements did not go unnoticed, which gave him the idea of making knives from scratch. He took part in his first knife show in 1968, where all of his models sold in record time.

He mixed with numerous artists in Chicago who encouraged the development of his aesthetic sense and instilled the principles of art in him, both in terms of form and strategy. He understood that if he wanted to make it in the cutlery trade, which was starting to get a little overloaded, then he would have to stand out from the competition through a completely original style.

So what was the young Lake specificity? The perfection of the fitting, the incomparable precision of the mechanism, the art of the interframe in fact. Instead of a "solid handle," that is to say instead of plaques of a chosen material fixed onto plates or miters placed at the front and back, the handle is produced in solid metal, but with wide gaps in which the decorative material is placed, either stag's antler or mouflon horn.

A Ron Lake knife is instantly recognizable, since the button for the switchblade mechanism is not placed conventionally on the back, but at the very end, in the form of a little lever. A precision mechanism, decorative appearance similar to a precious ornament and one-of-a-kind models that were very difficult to get hold of, Ron Lake's knives signaled the start of a new "art" cutlery.

Ron Lake.

Jay Hendrickson.

The art of inlaying

A perfect mastery of the art of inlaying.

When you're lucky enough to live just down the road from Bill Moran, how can you ignore what this genius bladesmith produces? The friendship that links these two men goes back a long way. It is almost a master/disciple relationship.

Moran reintroduced the art of embellishing a forged knife, taking his inspiration from the work of Black and Scagel. After having played with compositions of different materials, in the purest Scagel style, that is to say by sticking strips of leather between strips of stage antler, for example, or alternating with beautiful fruit-tree wood, Moran reinvented the art of inlaying. It took many years to find an inert wood, one that would not reject the silver thread. He finally found it with *curly maple,* which had the added advantage of having a very beautiful range of varying tones and patterns. Jay Hendrickson soon realized that he could never rival Moran as far as the forging of knives was concerned, since the results obtained by

Moran seemed to be more the fruit of genius rather than technique. However, Hendrickson was totally captivated by the art of decoration, and so that was where he was able to give full rein to his talent.

High quality blades, wonderfully worked handles, scrupulous attention given to the tiniest detail, such is the Hendrickson style. Naturally, the sheaths have not been forgotten; their leather is also decorated with the same motifs as those on the handle; sometimes there is one of those little "extras" so dear to Scagel, a silver arrowhead or star.

The tradition has thus been carried on, and Hendrickson, this worthy successor to Bill Moran, and head of the Association of American Master Smiths, will also become a legend himself, that's for sure.

Truly inspired by Moran but with that Hendrickson touch.

The African series

An original material for the handle, oosic.

A powerful blade for dealing with large African game, and a handle in sculpted ivory.

It is well known that Americans like to move around. Would this be due to the genes of their ancestors who, for the most part, traveled up and down the New World? Doyal Nolen makes his knives in Colorado from September to March, then in Texas from April to August, which provides him with a change of scenery. Between the two he goes even further, to assuage his consuming passion for big-game hunting, heading for Africa, as he has been doing for over ten years now. He thus knows what one expects of a good knife used in tough circumstances. Since 1968, when he started production, he has had the opportunity to experiment with various materials and perfect a multitude of models.

In homage to the continent whose vast expanses he has crossed, shouldering a powerful hunting rifle, he has designed a special "African series," using African materials for the handles. The blades are solid, sometimes finely worked or engraved, with all kinds of handles, from ivory to impala horn to all sorts of other trophy animals: gazelles, warthogs, buffaloes, gnus, etc. This great cigar smoker had already

been most innovative in his use of uncommon materials for handles, particularly roots of various trees, as well as oosic, which is neither more nor less than a fossilized walrus penis bone. That's originality for you! But Nolen also knows how to make knives of unbelievable simplicity for those particularly demanding customers, the hunters of Colorado, who are nevertheless obliged to be patient since you don't get served straight away here.

Doyal Nolen.

Various sculptures of grotesque faces decorate the handles of the knives.

Grotesque portraits

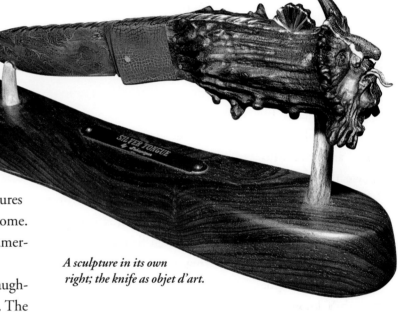

A sculpture in its own right; the knife as objet d'art.

H aving become an art in its own right, modern cutlery owed it to itself to take inspiration from all forms. At the time of the Renaissance, wall decorations using imaginative architecture or arabesques mixed with small figures were discovered in the buried remains of Ancient Rome. Ever since, this has been a source of inspiration for numerous artists and decorators.

Cathedral gargoyles, for example, provoked laughter through their extravagant or ridiculous appearance. The grotesque symbolizes a taste for the bizarre, for buffoonery and caricature.

James Schmidt is one of the very great bladesmiths to have followed in the footsteps of Bill Moran after the latter rediscovered damascene, and his reputation has rapidly gained the whole of the United States. He was the first to distinguish himself in grotesque art by carving a face into the rear end of his folding knives in stag antler.

Steve Schwarzer, who was his pupil, carried on the genre for a while before opting to concentrate on damascene, becoming famous for producing completely original designs, including mosaic. Steve was undoubtedly a pioneer in the working of materials and has certainly not finished astounding us.

Larry Fuegen, who forges extremely beautiful damascene, has always produced highly finished knives.

After trying his hand at sculpture, he made a considerable number of folding knives with stage antler handles, carving a grotesque face at their extremity. His name has become synonymous with this genre in which he fully intends to continue.

A second face, in case you didn't notice the first!

Three men in Colorado

Bill Sanders, a member of the Timberline trio.

The profession of bladesmith is generally a solitary one and the workshop is often built right in the middle of untamed nature as if to underline the fact. The extraordinary history of Timberline yet again illustrates this apparently ancestral rule.

Jim Hardenbrook worked alone in his little workshop at Cortez, his constant search for perfection earning him a solid reputation throughout the whole state of Colorado. When Vaughan Neeley, a young man from the area, expressed a desire to learn the trade, he couldn't have found a better master. In 1982, they formed a partnership, created Timberline Knives and set up their workshop in the San Juan Mountains. Situated high up, their chosen spot is not easily accessible in winter. The cabin in the middle of the forest is not very big, and there is no danger of any untimely

Well-designed finishes, like these micro-teeth opposite the cutting edge, and a guard cut from the blade piece.

visit, apart from the animals that inhabit the area. But that suited these two men just fine, who found there the tranquility and serenity that encourages energy and creativity. The adventure took yet another exciting turn when they were joined a few months later by a third man, Bill Sanders, already an established bladesmith in his own right.

The circumstances were perfect for nurturing a strong friendship between them. First, they had to travel together the distance separating Mancos, where they lived, from their workshop, with all the difficulties one might imagine. When it snowed, the only effective solution was to don snowshoes; then the entrance to the workshop had to be cleared with a shovel; finally, the wood fire had to be lit and kept going until the evening, and the return journey in the same epic conditions. How many times must they have been snowed in for several days and nights up there, unable to return to civilization?

Legend recounts that it is these exceptional circumstances that have favored the creation of their best models. The vast expanses of nature are certainly an incredible source of inspiration, but the danger is constant and drama frequent. In spite of being familiar with the area, Jim Hardenbrook fell to the bottom of a ravine during a storm.

A Timberline particularity:
accessories in the back of the sheath.

Timberline Knives comprises the most beautiful and luxurious catalog of handmade American cutlery ever printed. In a state where almost all of the inhabitants are hunters, the hunting range was of course the leading one with its mirror-polished blades giving superb cutting quality in any situation. Fishermen have not been forgotten, no less than outdoorsmen, for whom a folding survival knife was specially developed: the handle-plates can be taken off and the cavities have been designed to accept various accessories that one might need, such as a compass, matches, fishing line and hook, etc. In each sheath there is even a small accessory that might serve as an arrowhead, as well as a flint for making fires.

After Jim Hardenbrook's death in a hunting accident, the original Timberline split up to disappear into the mists and legends of the Rocky Mountains, but the brand still exists, albeit with a "factory" as opposed to a "custom" manufacture.

All of the models designed and produced during this first period in the little cabin in Colorado are very actively sought after by those knife collectors in the know; indeed there are now probably more of these collectors than there are models.

Handles containing
survival necessities.

A style all of his own

Frank Centofante.

This form of blade is typical of Centofante.

Thirty years in the profession and eight years as president of the prestigious American Knifemaker's Guild, the career of this craftsman from a family of Italian immigrants has been truly faultless. Frank Centofante learned knifemaking from his father in Florida. When he started in the profession in 1970, he made straight models that were not particularly original. At a knife show he met Bob Loveless, who fascinated him. He understood that in order to stand out from the competition he needed to develop a style all of his own. So he abandoned straight knives to devote himself to folding ones.

With Ron Lake the star of this genre, he took his inspiration from the latter's models, not for the interframe, which was quite difficult to produce, but for the type with the switchblade pump at the back of the handle.

For more traditional models he would place it conventionally on the back.

Since the shape of Loveless's blades were characteristic and very much in vogue, Centofante asked him to make him some that he could then mount on his folding frames. A series was thus developed with much success.

He then designed several models that affirmed his style before launching himself into the production of liner locks when they became fashionable, a genre that he would never leave.

His production was characterized by the quality of the mechanisms, a range of only a few models and selected materials for the handles, notably fossilized mammoth ivory.

In 1991, he left Florida to establish himself in Tennessee where his son joined him so that the Centofante style would carry on for many a long year.

Blades designed by Loveless and assembled by Centofante: highly sought after by collectors.

*The D'holder style; exquisitely beautiful,
but not just a pretty face…*

This is
"My knife"

When the knifemaking profession started to structure itself, through the impetus of Bob Loveless, there was only a handful of cutlers in the United States who worked to establish the Knifemaker's Guild in 1969. Dalton Holder soon joined them and such was his renown that he was elected president on an unprecedented two occasions, in 1982 and 1996! After spending his free time as a student "customizing" his friends' hunting knives in Texas, he started producing them as a hobby in 1968. His university education, combined with his work as sales manager for a major company and his passion for art—notably sculpture—were considerable assets when he launched himself into knifemaking full time.

His first creation, that has gone down to posterity, he simply called "My Knife."

Dalton Holder.

"My Knife" was a straight model whose handle was made of amber and oosic with brass divisions. This model was Dalton Holder's calling card, and he signed the blades "D'holder."

No one has ever copied him and for twenty-seven years orders from collectors have never stopped flowing in. Unable to build a reputation on a single model, he quickly designed a number of others, all of them straight, with a particularly robust blade and handle. However beautiful his knives may be, they are intended to be used.

As for his sheaths, he always uses the most beautiful leather, embossed with iron for a "basket" effect, and highly finished to the smallest detail, just like the knives that they contain.

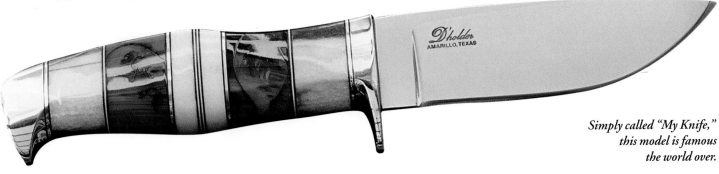

*Simply called "My Knife,"
this model is famous
the world over.*

The tradition of New Mexico

E ach State differs from its neighbor in certain ways, but if there is one which particularly stands out then it is certainly New Mexico! The contrasts are startling, whether in the landscape, climate or inhabitants, and the various cultures blend together in the most perfect harmony. In fact, it is more Mexico then North America through the architecture, clothes, and decoration. If one exercises the profession of knifemaker there then one is sure to stand out from the rest through one's style and way of working.

Although Harvey MacBurnette produces many fine straight knives, it is his folding models that have been particularly appreciated. The quality of materials, the precision of the mechanisms, and the robustness of the blades all contributed to his huge renown, but it is the shapes and decorations of Mexican inspiration that engender such admiration. Usually, a knifemaker limits himself to just making his knife. If he decides to embellish it with engravings or a scrimshaw, these tasks are then handed to the specialists in the material. MacBurnette, however, does it all himself: grinding, inlays, engravings, scrimshaw, etc. An all-round artist, admired by the whole profession, his knives are assiduously sought after by collectors. Even when he receives an order for a basic hunting knife, it will always be embellished with a most beautiful grinded finish.

If a knife is a MacBurnette then it certainly is a beautiful knife that will always be unique, standing out from any other!

Engravings and shapes of Mexican inspiration.

Harvey MacBurnette.

The engravings are always in perfect harmony with the shapes of the knife.

Pease

The preacher bladesmith

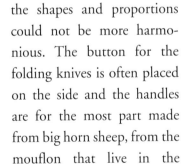

The switchblade button on the side and an incomparable handle.

Before turning their hobby into a full-time profession, most of the great knifemakers pursued other trades, whether that be carpenter, mechanic, lawyer, architect, chemist, engineer, or dentist. This was neither a handicap to their success nor a brake on their production. Moreover, when they become full time, either by choice or upon retirement, which is often at a relatively young age in Uncle Sam country, there is no visible sign of this change. One of the greatest American knifemakers is no dentist, lawyer or even engineer, but a preacher!

This unique fact is too original not to be underlined, and it is no secret for anyone, since at each Knife Show organized by the Guild a religious service is held on Sunday morning, and it is the Rev. William Pease who officiates, after which he takes off his preacher's clothes to sit behind a table on which are displayed a number of knives.

He has been a full-time knifemaker since 1978. He has

Bill Pease.

always made knives and started to earn his living from it in 1969. You can recognize a Pease from miles away: the mechanisms are perfect and the shapes and proportions could not be more harmonious. The button for the folding knives is often placed on the side and the handles are for the most part made from big horn sheep, from the mouflon that live in the Rockies.

For liner lock (linear switchblade) models, the miters are in blue-hued anodized titanium, as are the plates for maximum lightness. Preacher Pease's knives have already become a legend.

Titanium miters allow for a multitude of possibilities.

The Texan with simple tastes

Well rounded shapes which fit the hand well.

When you live in Waxahachie, a small Texan town of 15,000 souls, traffic jams and tall buildings hold little attraction, and as near as Dallas may be, one rarely goes there. Every bladesmith injects a little or a lot of his culture and way of life into his work. Warren Osborne has been exercising his profession full time since 1980, deciding to concentrate only on folding knives that have strong Texan influences. Producing knives for an essentially local clientele and at unbelievably low prices, he decided to see what was happening in town and, pushing himself a little, he didn't choose the smallest one: he went to New York where the annual Art Knife Show was taking place!

The welcome that awaited him must surely have surprised the cowboy in his Texan clothes: all the models on his table were sold in just a few hours! What was the reason for such success? Perfect finishing, original design, and very attractive prices! The meeting of Stetson and skyscraper enabled him to situate himself in relation to the market in general, although his modesty held him back a little. This experience gave him the opportunity to grow, to create other models and to go even further in the precision of the mechanisms, his choice of styles and diversity of materials.

He has naturally brought his prices up in line with his competitors, but needing little to lead a simple life, he now produces less.

An enthusiast of Japanese blades, he dreams of going to the Land of the Rising Sun to watch at work one of these legendary bladesmiths who has become a living national treasure.

Yes, this man is just like his knives: simple, but possessing the essential.

Pure Texan style from the good 'ole days.

Warren Osborne.

SIGMAN

A handle with rounded gaps for the fingers on both sides of the guard for a better grip.

A pillar of the Guild

Today, American bladesmiths are numerous. Each month sees new candidates present themselves; some last, others are just a flash in the pan. When the Knifemaker's Guild saw the light of day in 1969, its ranks were much more sparse and not many veterans of this golden era remain. One who is still going strong though is Corbet Sigman, whose renown in the 1960s was still in its infancy.

Shy, humble and modest, he is deeply respected by his peers; when one of them finds himself faced with a technical problem then it is to Corbet, and to him alone, that he turns.

He is an Old Master of all stages of the manufacture of a straight knife, something sufficiently exceptional to warrant a mention.

Corbet Sigman.

An illustration of his status comes from the magazine *American Blade,* which had the idea of publishing a book entitled *How to Make Knives.* It asked the best knifemakers to write about the stage of manufacture that they knew the best. Chapters were written by such prestigious names as Bob Loveless and Bill Moran. Only the "polishing" section remained; but to whom should it be entrusted? You guessed right, Corbet Sigman. But it could very well have asked him to write any other chapter. And we should not forget that when the Dutchman Frans van den Heuvel wanted to learn American cutlery techniques, it was Corbet Sigman he contacted,

who generously provided him with his advice by mail.

His straight knives are like him: robust, clear, simple and authentic, but what authenticity!

This is a typical Sigman shape.

C.R. SIGMAN

The quiet man

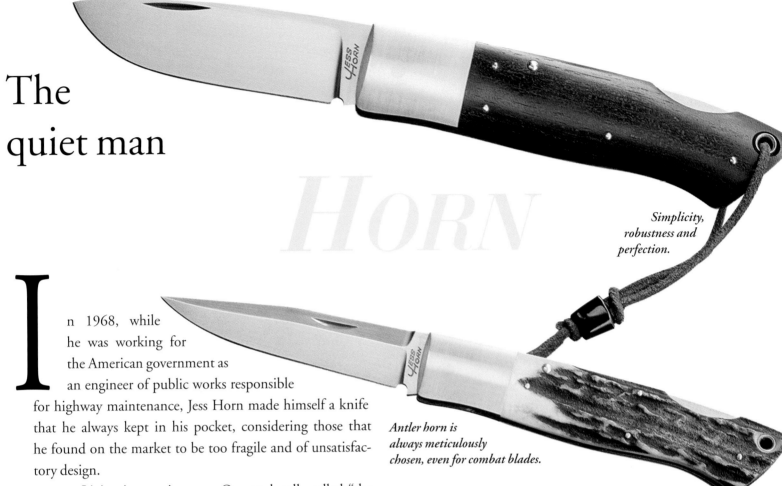

Simplicity, robustness and perfection.

Antler horn is always meticulously chosen, even for combat blades.

I n 1968, while he was working for the American government as an engineer of public works responsible for highway maintenance, Jess Horn made himself a knife that he always kept in his pocket, considering those that he found on the market to be too fragile and of unsatisfactory design.

Living in a region near Oregon locally called "the other California," Horn is of course a great devotee of fishing and hunting. For these activities he designed, but for a strictly personal use, very specific knives that suited him perfectly. But who out of his numerous hunting and fishing buddies could resist asking him to show them his knives, trying them out themselves and asking him to make identical ones for them? That is how Jess Horn started a small production for his close friends; but even in this huge country word gets around, and a number of retailers came along to place orders.

In Switzerland, Germany, and now in France, people tend to consider a Jess Horn to be the Rolls-Royce of knives. In the United States, he contradicts the saying that one is never a

Jess Horn.

prophet in one's own land, for his name ranks among the handful of top knifemakers specializing in folding knives. His knives are difficult to get hold of and delivery times are long, since our man is most meticulous in his work.

Jess Horn is a discreet man who will never admit having entered American cutlery legend and who continues to do his best work with the same models that are still as fascinating today as they were thirty years ago!

Jimmy Lile.

LILE

Rambo's supplier

F ashions come and go and knives are no exception. James B. Lile set up his bladesmith workshop in Russellville, Arizona, in the 1950s. Capable of making all kinds of knives, he was soon attracted by one in particular, the survival knife, which he started to produce in a variety of styles from the 1960s onwards. A pioneer of the genre, he built a solid reputation for himself particularly in the military.

Ever since John Nelson Cooper, no other knifemaker has been so solicited by the film industry. When the film *Rambo* was being shot, Sylvester Stallone, its star, needed to be armed with a combat and survival knife. Having heard of Jimmy Lile's talent, the man who would be known as Rambo asked him to design and manufacture a model that would be unique in its kind.

Thanks to Jimmy Lile, knifemakers renewed their contact with the movies kicking off a new and hopefully long collaboration, with many different craftsmen being asked to produce knives for other films, starting with Jack Crain for *Predator*.

The whole world was submerged by the survival knife craze, thanks to the movies, and this contributed to the rise in popularity of the art knife, particularly since

Jimmy Lile did not neglect to present a *"First Blood"* model to the president of the United States.

The name of Jimmy Lile has certainly become a legend, and although he passed away a few years ago, the man named "Gentleman Lile" by his peers left behind him other models that are no less famous, including a folding model with a completely new and patented blade-blocking system with an interframe handle.

Whenever this gentleman sold you a knife, he had the unforgettable particularity of warmly shaking your hand and, looking you straight in the eyes, pronouncing a "thank you" full of gratitude.

A patented mechanism and an original shape both contributed to the success of this beautiful folding knife.

The continuity of a name and a style

Over the years this basic concept has yielded numerous variations.

Each country has its household brands and knives are no exception. In the United States the all-conquering knife in question is a Murphy. David Zephaniah Murphy, born in Portland, Oregon, in 1895, produced a style of straight knife that would soon find its way into every American home. A blade forged in an excellent carbon steel with a simple handle, but one that had the particularity of being produced in molded aluminum. The knife was thus robust, light, cheap and didn't need special cleaning, which was why all housewives used it in their kitchens. Different shapes were produced for different uses, with models for hunters, scouts and butchers, etc.

Oregon, where nature is particularly wild, is a state with a strong knifemaking tradition and home of one of the greatest American knife manufacturers, Gerber. The firm's directors could not ignore the creative talent of the man whom his buddies called "Zeph," so they gave him a major order between 1938 and 1941. When World War II broke out soldiers needed to be equipped with combat knives. Gerber had already produced a high-quality range, but it was not possible to satisfy all of the requirements, and the models were costly to make. So Gerber once again called upon Zeph, who created a model using his already tried and tested methods: a robust blade and a handle with guard in molded aluminum. He made them for Gerber until 1941-1942.

In 1941 he created the "Murphy Combat Jr.," then in 1942 the "Murphy Combat," which was produced until 1945, all of them based on the same principle. Manufacture continued until 1954 and the country was soon inundated with them thanks to the vast stocks made for the army. His son David M., born in 1928 and who worked with his father until 1954, set up in Gresham where he continued working in the same tradition until his retirement in 1994. Up until then his advice had always been closely listened to by Gerber, whose slogan "legendary blades" has always rung true.

Dave Murphy.

*Powerful
folding
knives for
warlike
ends…*

*Bob
Terzuola.*

The South American influence

B ob Terzuola is a phenomenon, since he made his first knife when he was barely ten years old in his native village of Antigua, Guatemala. This passion for knifemaking has never left him, and after a military career where he learned under true battle conditions what a combat knife really was, he established himself in Antigua in 1980 as a knifemaker, specializing in the genre that he knew the best. Passionately interested in traditions and attracted by the legends of his own country, he chose the mysterious Mayan dragon as his logo. In 1982, he joined the famous American Knifemakers Guild before moving to New Mexico in 1984.

All of his models, whether for combat or outdoor activities, are astonishingly well studied down to the smallest details, including phosphate-coated blades to make them completely non-reflective. He innovated with sheaths in thermally molded Kydex, robust and imperishable, just like his micarta handles. Speaking several languages fluently, he has never hesitated to travel to Europe or Japan where his work has been unanimously appreciated, becoming a living legend as far as combat knives are concerned, even if his activities in South America and his relations with numerous guerillas are shrouded in mystery.

Contact with Frank Centofante, Ron Lake, Warren Osborne and Bill Pease nurtured a passion in him for the folding knife, and when the liner lock became popular, he started out making large combat models before producing a "cutthroat razor" model of the type much appreciated by sailors. And whenever he is asked for his source of inspiration he answers: "Perhaps a little from the Mayan dragon, but certainly a lot from good Bordeaux wine!"

*The Mayan dragon on a cutthroat razor
dearly loved by sailors.*

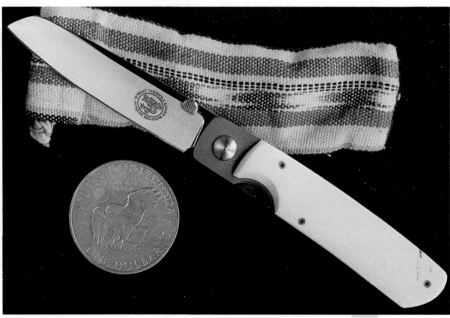

Two centuries of experience

The jewel of the brand, the impressive "Waidbesteck."

ORIGINAL
NACH OBERF
BEST. NO. 358

I n Europe, the great cutlery centers are few: Thiers in France, Sheffield in England, Maniago in Italy, Kauhava in Finland, Eskilstuna in Sweden and Solingen in Germany, which is where Johann Lauterjung got his brand registered by the town's Guild of Cutlers in 1769. Ever since then family members have succeeded each other in producing what has become the most prestigious German brand. The Puma name was adopted in 1860 at a time when exports were developing rapidly, not only to the whole of Europe, but also to the United States and to South America. The firm's production, which consisted of a range of good quality but common knives and razors, took a sharp turn at the end of World War II.

This "White Hunter" has been sold all over the world.

Franz Lauterjung and his son-in-law Oswald Ludwigsorf, a university graduate, acquainted with the latest technology and management methods were far from discouraged by the destruction of their factory in bombing raids. They had new premises built, acquired the latest equipment and hired the best personnel, even going as far as to organize training courses since qualified labor was hard to find in war-shattered Germany. They decided to devote the new range exclusively to hunting, fishing and outdoor activities, consisting of straight knives as well as many folding ones. These two enterprising fellows, themselves keen hunters and nature aficionados, realized that with the introduction of paid vacation, leisure activities would soon become an integral part of the new Germany, with outdoor activities leading the way and the vogue for camping also starting to grow. They immediately surrounded themselves with top hunting experts to develop knives suitable for all kinds of hunting.

And so, in collaboration with Mr. Frévert, inspector general of Water and Forests and also president of the International Federation of Hunting Dogs, the famous folding knife n° 959 was born, called the "Universal Jagdemesser." After equipping all German hunters, this model went on to conquer the world, and is still today considered as being the best of its kind. It consists of a main switchblade, a saw-toothed blade, a distended razor-blade model for disemboweling large game, a hook for gutting small poultry game, and a corkscrew. Building on its success, it was then made available in two, three and four pieces.

Old-fashioned charm.

Two efficacious blades for hunting.

present at each stage. The word "hand-made" that appears on each knife is thus not out of place.

While Puma manufactures everything that hunters need in terms of knives, anglers have not been forgotten. Once again models have been designed for all kinds of fishing and for all uses, with each detail and accessory the fruit of a long study undertaken by true specialists. If you consider their unparalleled quality of steel, "razor" sharpening and top-notch finish in all areas, you begin to understand why the brand has now been in existence for two hundred and thirty years!

Mr. Frévert was also responsible for many other models, notably a hunting-spear—the most beautiful one ever made—and the superb "Waidbesteck" collection, intended for handlers of bloodhounds. It spite of its age, this knife has never become outdated and 500 of them are produced each year.

Puma has a style all of its own, even a little antiquated, and a traditional method of manufacture. Despite high-technology tools, the hand of specialized workers is

From the revolver to the knife

Such finishing has never before been seen for a factory-made knife.

America is a huge continent, and from the date of its colonization until the end of 18th century, only part of the East was inhabited by the new arrivals. It was only at the beginning of the 19th century that the Europeans ventured into the real New World, that is to say over 10 million square miles of mountains, plains, forests, lakes, rivers and deserts. For such expeditions it was preferable to be in very good physical condition, not to venture off alone and to be well armed to deal with any attack, whether from Native Americans, outlaws or wild beasts, as well as being able to hunt for food. This generated a huge demand for the required weapons, and much progress was made in the design and production of firearms, despite the modest size of gun workshops in which three or four workers maximum would manufacture single pieces by hand.

It was only in 1820 that the American firearms industry really started. As for knives, they were mainly imported from England. It would be logical to think that this incredible knife market would have immediately interested the big firearm brands, but not at all. It was not until the beginning of the 20th century that some of them decided to turn their hand to it, while others waited even longer.

One of the brands that was almost synonymous with the legend of the Wild West was Smith & Wesson. Horace Smith and Daniel B. Wesson formed their company together in 1852 to make their famous revolvers. Blackie Collins was responsible for the first knives, designing a small series of an unbelievable beauty and perfect finish. They were certainly the most beautiful knives ever made by a firearms manufacturer. Of particular note were a Bowie knife commemorating the Texas Rangers, an outdoorsman, a survival model and a folding hunter. These creations are a part of history and of the prestigious company that is Smith & Wesson!

This folding model is similar to a hand-made knife.

A folding-knife with the miter in the shape of a guard was a totally new concept.

The legend of the Green Berets

Cultural blending can often produce astounding things. Born in the United States to a family of Chinese immigrants, the young Al Mar joined the Green Berets after having completed his university studies. Given his extraordinary physical capacities, he became a martial arts expert. Posted to South-East Asia with the special forces he experienced war at first-hand.

Upon returning to civilian life, he continued his studies of Far Eastern culture, obtained a diploma from a design school, practiced martial arts assiduously, and kept his shooting eye in.

Legend recounts that he was given numerous secret missions by the CIA, FBI and other services, but the man never talked about it. Always the knife enthusiast, he sat down and designed a whole series of combat models. He had the prototypes made and did the rounds of special forces units, police forces, coast guards, border guards, the FBI and the CIA in order to consult the relevant specialists.

Such approaches would seem to confirm that he had contacts in the "top secret" services and since there is never smoke without fire… At any rate, he went to see the best Japanese manufacturer, the Sakai company, and the first models went on the market. The success was immediate, with professionals able to have nothing but confidence in this experienced man, decorated in combat.

And so the range was extended, in both straight and folding models, with all genres considered, from hunting, to fishing, to outdoor activities, etc.

A red logo symbolizing a warrior, like those used in Chinese calligraphy, was struck on each blade so that there would be no ambiguity as to whom it was intended for.

Although he has now passed on to join his ancestors, Al Mar was a true legend in his lifetime.

Al Mar designed all kinds of folding models.

Legend and reality

*The cover
of an old catalog
of the brand.*

I n the United States, "Buck" is almost synonymous with "knife," which says a lot about this brand. Such renown can be better understood if we look at the history of this great company that has clearly become a legend. Hoyt Buck became an apprentice metalsmith at the age of ten. The year was 1899, the place was Kansas City, Missouri.

Amazingly, only three years later—he had just turned thirteen—he perfected a new process for thermally treating carbon steel, which gave the latter hitherto undreamed of qualities. He kept this discovery strictly to himself though.

At eighteen years old, he quit and started a new life of travel and odd jobs. He was first of all drawn to the sea, and then to Daisy, whom he married. Al, their first son, was born in October 1910, followed by six other children.

*An infinite range
of straight models was
manufactured along
the lines of this design.*

But whatever profession he exercised, Hoyt was never far from a forge and he regularly made knives in his spare time that he sold to his acquaintances.

Al inherited his father's passion for the sea and joined the U.S. Navy.

Upon returning to civilian life, Al discovered religion and left for Chicago with his brother George to join a Bible school. But without much money, the voyage was long and difficult, and in the meantime, the school had closed!

He certainly never thought that he would one day exercise the profession of knifemaker and that right next to the lake lived the best bladesmith in the country, Bill Scagel, whom he had never met.

From 1941 his father started to make knives regularly by hand with whatever tools he could find in his new house in San Diego. Every morning he made the tour of his neighbors, the sports shops and gunsmiths to try and sell the few knives he made. Al started helping him in 1947.

The Buck Knife Co. got off to a lightning start, with Hoyt using all of the ingenuity and skill that he had gathered since a little boy. The tempering secret that he had discovered as a thirteen-year-old, and which was the secret of the brand's renown, he passed on to Al, who passed it on to Chuck, the present guardian of the Hoyt name.

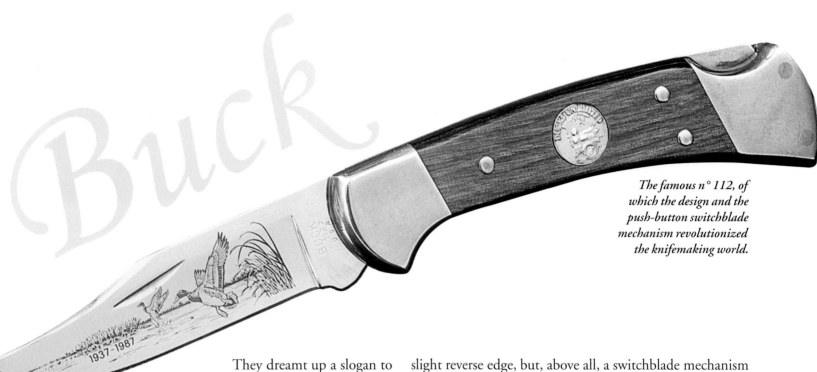

Buck

They dreamt up a slogan to convince the hesitant buyer, with a logo showing a hammer striking a blade whose cutting edge rests on the top of a nail placed on an anvil. The text reads: "The knife that splits nails!" At this time, shock slogans really pulled all the stops out…

Buck stands for quality of steel and an extremely vast range, but it is also a recognizable style, with innovations that marked the cutlery world and shook it up more than once.

Up until then, knives, whatever the brand, lacked a switchblade system. On the 7th of November 1965, an historic day, the model n° 110, called the "Folding Hunter," was launched on to the market. Its particularity? An even more distinct style, namely a handle composed of two wooden plaques fixed between two brass plates and a powerful blade with a tapering point and a slight reverse edge, but, above all, a switchblade mechanism with the button on the back of the handle. The n° 112 or "Ranger," which soon followed, was of identical design but shorter.

The popularity of these models was without precedent, and Buck's competitors were obliged to follow in their footsteps, modifying their production to include this new switchblade that everyone was demanding. Buck is always on the lookout for new developments to remain firmly in step with, or even slightly ahead of, its time.

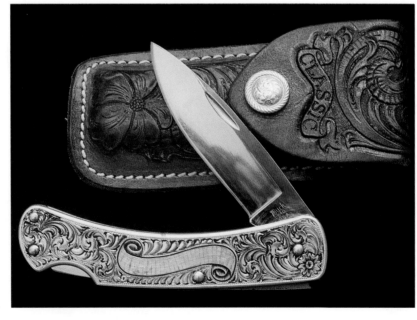

The inspiration of the Old West.

Legendary blades

These folding knives are among the most appreciated.

In 1939, when the Gerber brand saw the light of day, a slogan was immediately chosen that would point the way: "Legendary blades." It was a daring claim, but one it lived up to. The brand has reached all five continents with its reputation fully intact.

Established in Oregon, the brand was naturally responding to local demand when it launched its first range. With American troops engaged in World War II, a "combat" series was quickly developed.

But it was not until the advent of the Vietnam War that the most effective models were created, notably the famous "Mark II" dagger.

Gerber has been consistently innovative in all areas, thus standing out from all the other manufacturers, even ones that are much older; firstly through an extremely wide range for every use, with both straight and folding models; secondly by an irreproachable quality, steels that can stand anything, cutting edges that are as fearsome as they are durable, a style all of its own and a robustness that is particularly appreciated; finally, and this is perhaps its greatest originality, by a close collaboration between the greatest

A hunting model with a superb finish.

names in hand-crafted knifemaking, something that had never been seen before.

The first knifemaker whose services were requested was David Murphy—his workshop was not far away—who provided judicious advice concerning the choice of steel and tempering processes, and who gave his opinion concerning each new model as it came off the drawing board. The second was a talented designer, Blackie Collins, who designed a multitude of models all destined for great success. The third man was Bob Loveless, who designed blades for mounting on existing models. In view of the reputation of this genius bladesmith among knife collectors, the opportunity of procuring his famous signature at an affordable price was too attractive to pass up. The famous Colonel Rex Applegate also left his indelible mark on the combat models.

Gerber certainly merits its slogan of "Legendary blades!"

There were many folding knives, all of them designed differently.

Cutting edge

The first members of the Kershaw family were trappers in Oregon, that state where wild nature has the edge, since it is as large as half of France but with only three million inhabitants. A ranch was built that was used from generation to generation. In 1939, the prestigious Gerber brand set up its premises not far from that property.

The young Pete Kershaw, who worked his way through many knives, his activities in this untamed nature seriously putting blades to the test, now started to supply himself directly at the "factory," where he became well-known.

The directors of Gerber knew a good opportunity when they saw it and so got Kershaw to start testing new steels and prototypes. He was thus able to familiarize himself with the various stages of manufacture. But much as he appreciated Gerber's production and their prestigious quality, the style of the range did not appeal to him in its entirety.

Unable to persuade Gerber to adopt the shapes that he suggested, he started to sketch all of his ideas out on paper. In the 1970s with the Vietnam War in full swing, Gerber was concentrating all of its production on military models.

So Kershaw decided to produce his own knives, but without compromising his quality of life in the great outdoors. He designed a whole line, contacted Kai in Japan for the manufacture, and took charge of the distribution himself. He innovated a completely new style that was an immediate success, with much attention paid to the finish and mounting, as well as the quality of the cutting edges, that soon made the name of the new brand.

His catalog have continued to progress over the last twenty-five years, while the leading models of the first few years remain imprinted in the memory of the hunters who used them.

Kershaw…a totally new style.

Fearsome teeth

Who would have thought that it would still be possible to innovate in an area as traditional as knifemaking? Yet to the great surprise of the profession and its clientele the spider brand has done just that. More revolution than evolution. But let's see how…

Sal Glesser sold grindstones out of the back of a baker's delivery truck. Sharpening no longer held any secrets for him and as he made his way up and down the country, all kinds of knives passed through his hands, eventually giving him the idea of making one himself from a completely originally design. The year was 1981 and he called it the "Worker." As he obviously intended to make others he gave it the code "CO1." This first model was quite original in a number of ways.

Sal had noticed that not only was it easy to lose a knife that you just slipped in your pocket, but it was also difficult to get hold of it. And while working it was necessary to put down whatever you were holding in order to have both hands free to open the blade. Last but not least, it had to be robust in every area, considered as a tool in its own right.

The handle was produced in metal for robustness. A metal clip was screwed to it so that it could be put somewhere accessible and kept securely in place. That way the knife could be clipped to a pocket, for example. As for the opening of the blade, a decent-sized hole was pierced at the point where one would normally expect to find the thumbnail groove; the blade could thus be opened by using the thumb of the hand holding the knife. In short, everything could be done with one hand! A simple enough idea and obvious when you think about it! Add to that an excellent steel for the blade so as to obtain a durable and high-quality cutting edge, and a new genre was born. But reception of this first model was mixed: some considered it a work of genius and adopted it

A micarta handle replaces steel on many models.

This "Toad" is signed Dalton Holder.

straight away, while others rejected it for being too heavy and cold.

But the project for a "Clipit" series, carrying the "Spyderco" brand, was still in its infancy, and the thunderbolt came the following year with the "Mariner" model. The concept was rigorously identical, with only the shape and size changing. The great innovation was to design a blade without a traditional cutting edge, but completely sawtoothed! Blades with sawteeth had existed for a long time, first of all for hunting knives, then for diving knives and finally survival knives. There already existed a multitude of tooth types, from the very fine to the very wide, on one row or in two staggered rows, but the originality of Spyderco was to propose a quite unusual form: three small teeth alternating with wide, deep teeth, and a beveled edge on

one side. This was a major development, since this design of cutting edge was incredibly effective. After having patented the clip and the principle of the hole pierced in the blade, Spyderco naturally took out a patent for this kind of teeth, which of course became a house specialty. This time it had universal success; the Clipit became the essential knife and sold like hotcakes all round the world.

Ever since, the range has developed considerably and the catalog grows from year to year. An extremely wide variety is now on offer, with lighter handles in micarta, Zytel, carbon fiber, fiberglass, G 10, Craton and even titanium. The best steels are always selected for the blade, enabling effective combinations, with the teeth on one side of the blade, for example, or a traditional cutting edge for those who are not fans of novelty.

The spider has not finished weaving its web, with the best craftsmen being asked to design special models: Jess Horn, Frank Centofante, Bob Terzuola, Dalton Holder, etc. And since Spyderco is always keen to veer off the beaten track, it is never afraid to call on the services of original bladesmiths, like Eduard Bradichansky, who wishes to bring into line with modern tastes the "shabaria," a strangely shaped dagger carried by the nomads of the Jordan valley many centuries ago.

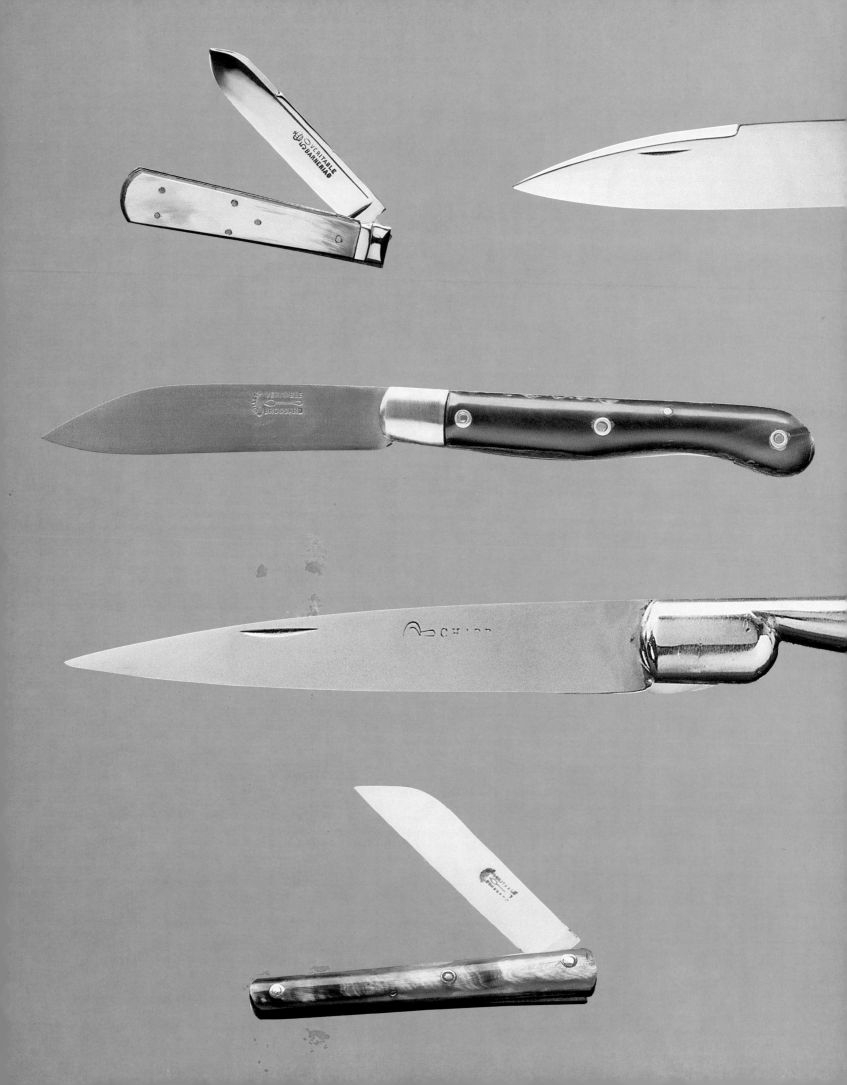

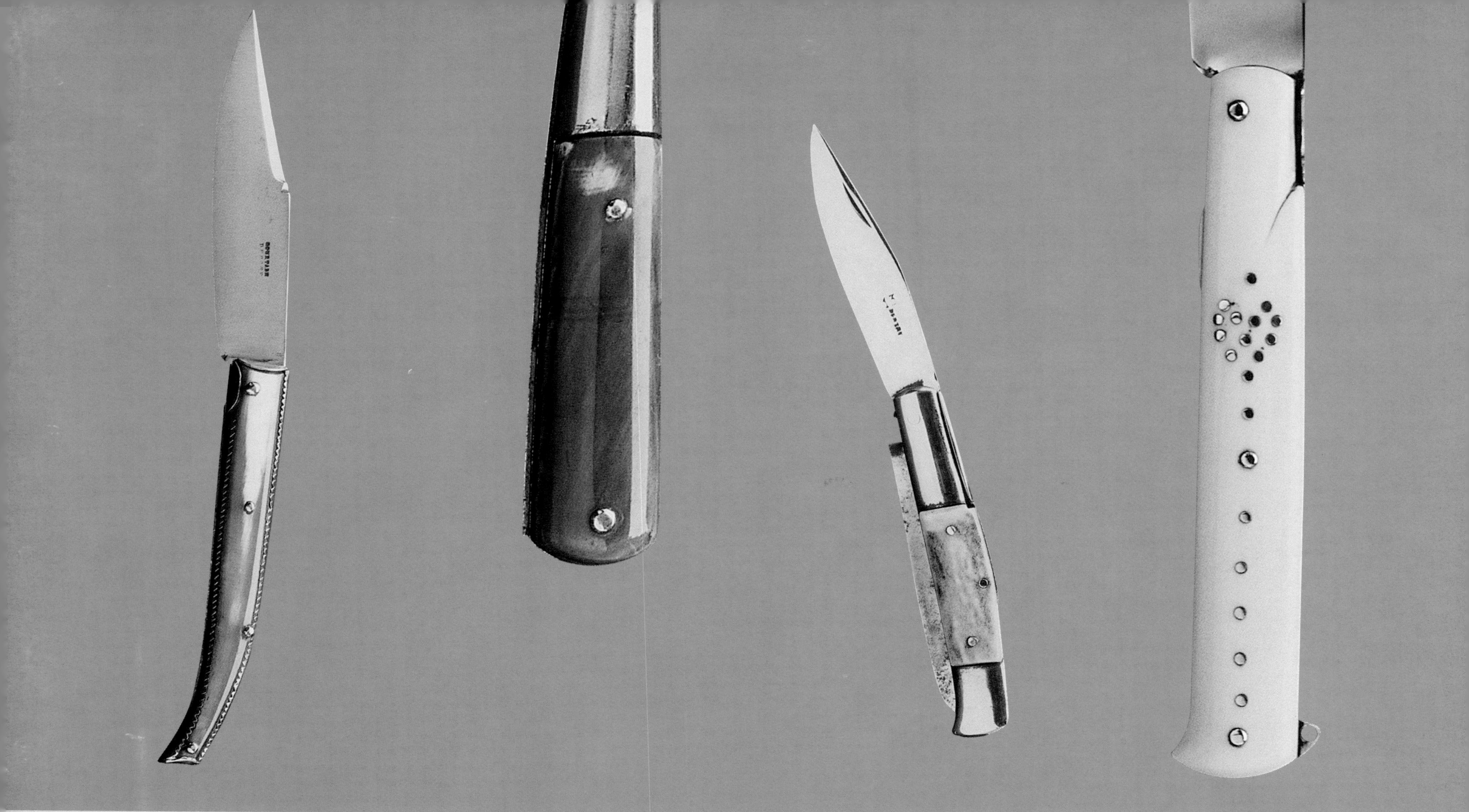

Traditional knives

Precursor of a long line

I t is too often forgotten that the study of prehistory is a science of essentially French origin dating from the 19th century, despite the few allusions to it made by Greek and Roman authors. In the 16th century it was discussed by Mercati, and Jussieu published a paper on the subject in 1723, but their only merit was to evoke the hypothesis of there having existed very ancient civilizations, but without citing a single fact or discovery, let alone any dates.

It was Boucher de Perthes who clearly spoke of the existence of prehistory, that is to say the science of the life of humanity before the development of writing, following which research was undertaken on various sites by Edouard Lartet and then Gabriel de Mortillet. To the latter we owe the classification that is today considered as the benchmark for French

prehistory: chelléen, moustérien, aurignacien, solutréen, magdalénien, etc. De Mortillet didn't choose these names at random: they correspond precisely to the areas in France where the most characteristic archaeological layers where laid bare and in which fundamental discoveries were made.

Scientists have not finished scouring the world searching for the tiniest piece of evidence enabling them to determine the epoch and location of what they call the "cradle of humanity." Yves Coppens considers it to lie in the part of the Rift Valley that runs through East Africa, where the remains of "Lucy" were discovered, a 3.3 million year-old woman…Michel Brunet, who found the jawbone of "Abel," is more in favor of Chad…

What is not in doubt, however, is humanity's family tree, that is to say the various types of human who have peopled the world, as well as each one's place on the evolutionary ladder.

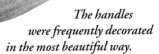

The handles were frequently decorated in the most beautiful way.

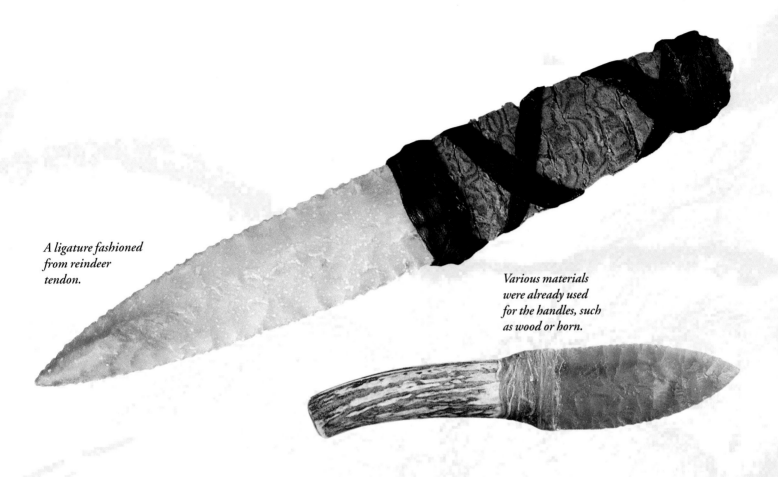

A ligature fashioned from reindeer tendon.

Various materials were already used for the handles, such as wood or horn.

So it was in the first Paleolithic period that the first techniques for hewing flint developed, with two stones being struck violently against each other. At this time, our ancestors had discovered fire and hunted large game. The various periods succeeded each other, technology developed, and from the simple shard of flint grasped in one's hand, we arrived at much more sophisticated objects, particularly in the Mesolithic age, the great reindeer hunting period. Not only was it the peak of the bone-working age, since we have found numerous objects in this material, particularly harpoons and needles, but it was also the greatest period for the hewn stone industry.

But although there is no argument that Professor Raymond Art discovered the first Australopithecus in Southern Africa in 1925, it is in the Périgord (France), however, that the most important prehistoric site lies. Here is where the most remarkable remains have been found, as well as sites that gave their name to science. Micoque for the

micoquien period, Moustier for the moustérien period, Madeleine for the magdalénien period, etc. The digs have enabled precious treasures to be brought to light: cave paintings, sculptures and jewels, as well as tools, hunting weapons and of course knives, including these marvelous willow-leaf shaped knives, of which we still don't know whether they are utilitarian objects or stylistic creations, as well as bows and amazing flint knives. We have not really been able to invent anything better since: a blade mounted on a handle, whose material varies considerably, and frequently finished in a particularly artistic way. Even all those years ago, beauty and originality were already highly prized, not to mention practicality, since almost all of the parts of dead animals served a purpose: tendons, bones, leather, teeth, wood or horn, all were used for technical ends. With wood and stone being used as well, it is clear that craftsmen at the time had an abundant variety of materials at their disposal, and that they were not short of ideas.

Simplicity in its purest form

Example of a primitive knife par excellence, although somewhat sophisticated as far as the thumb support is concerned.

T he first modern folding knife is generally known as the "primitive knife" because of its design, which has been much copied since. The blade is made of steel and the handle of stag's antler, although it can also be made of bone, ivory, horn or wood. The handle is split so as to receive the blade when it is folded. The blade swivels on a pin at the top of the handle, with the heel of the blade fitting into a groove in the top of handle so as to keep it straight when open. The fundamental difference between this blade and a more modern design is that there is no spring to keep the blade either open or closed, which means that it is not particularly secure. Wear and tear also take their toll on pins and grooves.

But the designers of this knife were still pretty ingenious, fitting a piece of steel onto the heel of the blade, onto which the user could exert pressure with their thumb to prevent the blade from closing on their fingers during use.

The principle of a blade swiveling on a pin and folding into a handle is as old as the hills, maybe older! The Romans were already producing knives of this design, although the idea of prolonging the heel of the blade with a piece of steel is more recent. It would seem that the first models of this type appeared in Louisiana in the 18th century. Since Louisiana was a French colony at the time, it is quite possible that the designer of this knife was a Frenchman, perhaps a descendant of the flint-tool makers of the Périgord.

Judicious marriage of the past and the present: a damascene blade for a better cutting-edge, and a ring so as not to lose it.

The handles were frequently decorated with magnificent scrimshaws.

The knife of the first Native Americans

When Christopher Columbus set foot on the shores of America in 1492, the continent was already inhabited by five million individuals. The first known Native Americans, of whom some extremely interesting remains have been found, lived in Mexico around 14,000 B.C. and were given the name Clovis. Their sites overflow with thousands of objects, including spearheads, scrapers and blades in stone, bone or ivory. This perfectly organized civilization has left us the most ancient and most abundant archaeological heritage of the American continent, and it is interesting to note that certain blades were made from flint, and others from obsidian.

Flint is a very hard siliceous rock, composed of chalcedony, quartz and opal, forming nodules in certain limestone rocks. Obsidian, which looks like glass, is a rock formed from different types of flowing lava produced by erupting volcanoes.

These various types include andesite, which is either gray (diorite family) or black (gabbro family); diorite, which is a granite rock formed from feldspar crystals; gabbro, which is a granular pyroxene based rock; rhyolite, of granite composition and with a vitreous appearance; porphyry, which is dark red and a variety of andesite; and trachyte, which is particularly hard to the touch.

Obsidian was not hewn by striking it, like with flint, but by using pressure, a most difficult operation. The blades thus obtained had a cutting power comparable to the best steel, which enabled fearsome knives and arrowheads to be fashioned. These blades were mounted on antler stage handles decorated according to the customs of the various tribes.

Curiously though, obsidian, a material that comes to us out of the mists of time, was not only used by the Indians in the prehistoric era, but also up until the second half of the 19th century, even though metallurgy had existed on other continents since 3,000 B.C.

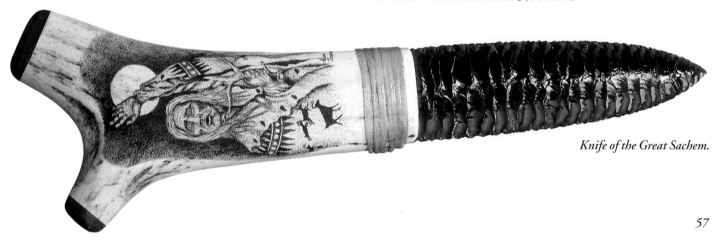

Knife of the Great Sachem.

The knife for unsealing letters and sharpening quills

…and even for scratching off dried quills

With a long blade requiring a long handle, the letter-opener is not really a pocket knife…

Before the relatively late appearance of the metal-nib pen, natural quills were used, selected from the biggest wing and tail feathers of certain fowl, principally goose. The essential accessory for a quill pen was a penknife, originally straight, with a single, very fine and quite short blade that was used to shape and sharpen the point and make a slit, just like modern metal nibs, which permitted upstrokes and downstrokes; it was also used to scratch off any dried ink on both sides of the nib.

The more it was used, the more uses were found for it… scratching away ink on the paper, for example, to get rid of a stain or correct a mistake. Numerous expressions were born of its use, such as to "cut out" something in a piece of text. In the past it was quite a common practice to use a penknife to literally "cut" a word or phrase "out" of a contract or other text.

Later on, the folding penknife became more widespread, to which was added a second blade, much longer and thicker than the first, intended for opening a letter, whether by cutting off the wax seal or slicing open the gummed-down paper. Since this was an accessory for the aristocracy, it was inconceivable that it would not be as elegant as possible. Cutlers rivaled each other in their ingenuity and talent in their choice of shapes, materials and engravings.

The collection exhibited at the City Museum in Sheffield, England, is quite edifying, when one considers the incredible luxuriousness of certain models, but those on show at Thiers, Langres or even Nogent are not bad either.

Any person of importance had one of these knives. George Washington received a knife with a mother-of-pearl handle when he was only fifteen years old, and which he always kept with him; it has been on exhibition since 1812 in the George Washington Masonic National Memorial in Alexandria, Virginia.

With the blade folded the knife can be carried easily.

From the pruning knife to the small folding sickle

I f there is one particular set of professions for which a considerable number of knives have been developed, then it is clearly the agricultural and related professions. Each knife corresponds to a specific use and has been designed as a real tool.

The grafting knife is particularly well known, the grape-harvest knife less so. When one evokes grape harvests one imagines the carriers on one side, with their huge baskets on their backs, the cutters on the other side armed with a kind of secateur and the vine in the middle. However, the secateur is a relatively recent apparition, preceded by the pruning knife. Small sickle or pruning knife, the name is particularly evocative…

The first legendary users were the druids, who cut mistletoe according to an ancestral rite, even going as far as to use golden blades, not only to imbue their ceremonies with greater prestige, but also so as not to soil their precious harvest that was destined to undergo an alchemical procedure supposed to bestow magical powers upon it.

The traditional sickle was used to cut grass, wheat, rushes and various other plants. Grapes were thus harvested using a small sickle. Since it was not reserved strictly for this use, it had to be more compact; it was also straight, that is to say the curved blade extended from the handle. Since it is not exactly easy to carry around a sickle, not to mention risky, the idea for a much smaller and folding sickle soon gained ground before finally seeing full development at the end of the 19th century.

The grape-harvest knife was thus born, with the blade folding into the handle, easily carried in one's pocket and generally manufactured by local craftsmen. Having been knocked off its perch by the secateur, it is now coming back into vogue in numerous wine-producing regions, particularly Bordeaux.

The folding pruning knife, ancestor of the grape-harvest knife.

Shiny metal for easy retrieval

Particularly robust, but light to carry.

What remains today of this profession, but the occasional delivery horse and cart used by long-established companies to evoke the traditional standing of their firm (several breweries in London, England, for example). Yet these vehicles performed sterling services, carrying a huge variety of goods. After the Great War, everything had to be rebuilt from zero, at least in Europe, and it was often difficult to find material and infrastructure that were up to the task. Whether in capital cities, towns or the countryside, carts were everywhere to be seen, and horses and their drivers had their work cut out. A carter's day was usually long and he had to eat when and where he could, which often meant on the roadside or in a local diner. They all carried a knife in their pocket, a knife made in Thiers, inexpensive and which soon earned the sobriquet of "carter's knife," in view of its great popularity in this profession.

The old established Thiers firm *A l'étoile d'acier*, like many others at the time, faced a significant lack of raw materials, but there was a considerably large stock of aluminum, copper, brass and steel that now had to be used for other purposes than the armaments industry for which it had originally been earmarked.

This knife was composed of a large blade, in "Piétain," another smaller one, and sometimes a saw. The sides were produced either in aluminum or brass, depending on what was available. The knife was thus light, yet robust, since both aluminum and brass are fairly resistant to shock and scratches. In addition, the fact that these materials shone in the sun made them easier to retrieve if dropped or mislaid.

This do-it-all knife was produced up until 1940, after which it disappeared, just like the profession it had served so well.

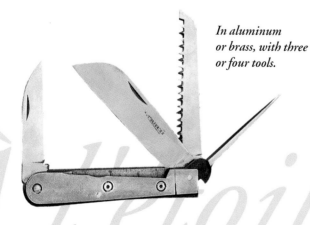

In aluminum or brass, with three or four tools.

À l'étoile d'acier

Certain straight models even had a spoon-shaped plate to gut fish with.

A tool for every purpose

T he fishing world is simply fascinating, starting with its multitude of accessories: split-reed or carbon-fiber rods, reels—from the simplest to the most sophisticated—clothes, boots and hats of all kinds, flies—each one more beautiful than the last—and knives to deal with any situation! Just like hunting, fishing provides a myriad of possibilities!

You tend to eat next to your rod, the float bobbing in the water, so you need a good knife to cut great hunks of that wonderful farmhouse bread on which you might spread delicious potted meat, for example. You also have to fix ballast to the line in different weights, cut that impossibly resistant nylon line, and re-trim the hook after it got bent askew during the previous struggle with a huge catch that eventually got away... Having finally caught a fish, you need to scrape off its scales, gut it and possibly even disgorge it.

So certain anglers choose a folding multi-blade model that allows them to do all of this at once. It has a sufficiently large main blade, a shorter one, a pair of miniature pliers, a scale-scraper, a disgorger, and a small pair of scissors, as well as the essential corkscrew and bottle-opener. But these knives, which are often cheap, are not always of the greatest quality,

and many prefer other models with fewer tools but more effective.

A straight knife, for example, with a good blade in the heel of which a V-shaped notch with sharpened sides has been placed, allows one to cut a nylon line with ease. In addition, the handle has a spoon-shaped piece of metal on the end of it that serves to gut the fish.

Certain folding models from reputable brands are also very good, but for robustness the number of blades is generally limited to two: one long, fine and pointed blade, with teeth on the back for scraping the scales, and another one that serves as a disgorger, for example. You can even find models that have a handle equipped with a sharpening stone for hooks.

Folding knife containing the essentials, including a sharpening stone.

Essential for all rural bleeding operations…

A whole kit contained in a case.

The vet's knife has a quite original appearance. For a long time, the practice of bleeding animals was an extremely common little surgical operation (for humans too) that was known from ancient times. The operation was carried out on an area of healthy tissue and consisted of evacuating a certain quantity of blood by an opening made in an artery, vein or capillary using a simple instrument. There is documentary evidence of laws and decrees, dating from 1762, authorizing certain professions to practice this simple surgery on horses, cows and sheep: farriers, healers, horse-dealers, cattlemen, shepherds, carters, horsemen and, of course, vets.

The cutlers of Thiers soon responded to this professional demand by coming up with the ideal instrument that they called the "flamme" (literally: flame). This type of tool can be found from the 18th century up until the start of the 20th century, and such longevity can be explained not only by a boundless faith in the virtues of this practice, but also by its simplicity and the number of professionals qualified to undertake the operation.

The "flamme" looks like a sort of arrowhead placed perpendicular to the end of a shank. The practitioner would select a "flamme" of a greater or lesser size according to requirements, which is why these vet's knives never had less than three differently-sized ones. And since the scalpel was another surgical instrument that was often needed, one or several of them, straight or curved, were also included in the set. Finally there was also a scraper for cleaning animals' feet.

Six-piece vet's knives were thus common, the parts swiveling in and out of a metal case, allowing for easy transport, with one instrument bring used at a time.

There are even personalized luxury models.

The peeler was a truly great invention!

Unimaginable

T he major brands of the Thiers cutlery industry are numerous and often quite old; the Thérias family is one of them; its trademark "le Parapluie à l'épreuve" (literally: the umbrella put to the test) depicting the outline of an opened umbrella was registered on the 26th of March 1819. Up until 1970, they made mainly folding knives, but from this date onwards they started to make kitchen knives and then professional knives, like the "Unique Sabatier," for example. When marketing these new models to the meat and food professions, they soon realized that there was quite an interesting market niche that was not to be overlooked, that of accessories for professional cooks. Since there was already a brand that had made its name with famous peeler, the "Econome," they decided to get into partnership with it and even merge. So Thérias and Econome set out to satisfy the needs of all cooks both professional and amateur.

This was how the famous Econome became known all over the world, was improved upon, variations produced and other utensils designed and produced so as to make tasks easier, even pleasant. The firm's catalog is today impressive, and when you feel like cutting loose in the kitchen, a chef's hat jauntily sitting on your head, you can't ignore the amazing range that they offer. There are no less than sixteen different peeler models, zesters (single, double, right-handed and left-handed, etc.) knives for apples, tomatoes, pineapples, grapefruit, and lemons, whether for cutting, scraping them out or decoratively slicing them, and not to mention all of the knives for fish, meat, bread, butter…

The Thérias name is already legendary, and the Econome, for which all those appointed to potato peeling duty will be forever grateful, will doubtless become a part of that legend.

Knives and utensils for all domestic uses.

Nearly two centuries in the kitchen

If there is a knife the reputation of which has flown far beyond the French borders, to the extent that it has become considered as a true ambassador of France in professional butchery and cooking circles all over the world, then it is certainly the Sabatier! The story begins at the start of the 19th century, in Bellevue, in the Thiers suburbs, where a certain Philippe Sabatier made knives for professionals. The success was such that he was obliged to place a trademark on the knife to distinguish it from those of his competitors: this mark was a "K," and so the "Sabatier K" was born in 1810.

The blade, made from carbon steel, came in different lengths, with the handle mounted on the tang. His son, Bonnet, who succeeded him, used the same brand. His two sons, Gabriel and Pierre, after having worked with their father, established their own company called "Sabatier Frères," before going their separate ways.

Gabriel continued under the name "Sabatier Aîné" (literally: "Senior") using the "K" brand, and Pierre under the name "Sabatier Jeune" (literally: "Junior") using the crowned "K" brand.

But why was this knife such a success, both in France and throughout the world? The answer lies in its quality and equilibrium, its weight and balance in the hand being much more effective and pleasant than what one could find up until then. In addition, although there was nothing particularly original about the shape of the blade, it was available in varying lengths, heights and thicknesses, an undoubted innovation that did not go unnoticed by their clientele.

The models do not all follow the same design, so as to meet different requirements.

Sales were local at first, at agricultural fairs, but since cooking professionals were very geographically mobile, they did not hesitate to travel all the way to Thiers to get themselves equipped with the same blades as their colleagues. Knife retailers also came from all over the country to stock up, which explains the success at a national level. All that remained was to conquer the other continents, which was undertaken thanks to a well-conceived export policy.

Any object that becomes legendary can only be copied, and that was how the knife came to be made by a multitude of other brands, right up until today: Bonnet Sabatier, Sabatier 62 and Sabatier 65, with trademarks as diverse as an anvil, a lion, a diamond, a trumpet, an elephant, the "True," and who knows how many others... Each manufacturer had their own characteristics as far as materials, manufacturing methods and design were concerned. Certain knives were forged, others cut. Steel was either carbon or chrome, which made it stainless.

In the beginning, blade and miter were a single piece, with a molded handle fixed with three characteristic rivets. The range was of course generously extended to include numerous other models, so that professionals could deal with any situation, whether that be cutting up meat, fish or vegetables. It enabled sets to be marketed containing the whole "Sabatier" range, with each type of knife being made according to the same criteria of quality and robustness.

It would take a smart guy to say which was the best out of all these brands, but what is certain is that everyone can find a Sabatier to suit his hand.

Philippe could never have imagined that this knife, which he designed and manufactured in 1810, would become a legend, garner such fame throughout the world and still be around two centuries later. At the start of the third millennium, Sabatier knives still have a wonderful future ahead of them.

The Sabatier in all its simplicity.

Knights and their ladies were already aficionados

Even today, the great brands have not neglected the penknife handle, which they have modernized.

Metal handles are well suited to numerous designs.

In the French language, this is called a "canif." If we go back to 1441, we find that this word was spelled "knif" and pronounced "k-nif." We can clearly see that in the reverse of the major French influence on the English language, after William the Conqueror and his Norman followers invaded England in 1066, here is a word of clear Anglo-Saxon origin that has jumped back over the Channel!

Through the 15th, 16th and 17th centuries, the word was even pronounced "ganif" in certain regions where the "c" was replaced by a "g." In 1650, Gilles Ménage, to whom we owe the *Origins of the French language,* that etymological study later developed to form the first great French etymological dictionary, recommended that the word should be pronounced "ganif." But two-hundred years later, Emile Littré, in his dictionary written between 1863 and 1873, insisted that the word be pronounced canif, which he found to be more modern.

The definition of the word has also varied according to the era. The most interesting one is that given by Jean-Jacques Perret,

author of *The Art of Cutlery,* dating from 1771: "canif – instrument for sharpening quills; there are several types, straight and folding ones."

Camille Page, in the monumental work that he wrote in 1896, *Cutlery from its Origins to the Present Day,* used more or less the same definition, while in the 20th century, encyclopaedias defined it as being a "small pocket knife, with one or several blades folding into the handle."

So the penknife is a small folding knife, the first examples of which were used to shape and sharpen goose quills.

The cutlery experts of Paris and Nogent made this knife a specialty of theirs, and they produced numerous versions of it for men's pockets or women's handbags, with one or several blades and various accessories.

The typical penknife, with nail file and decorated sides. There is a vast array of different designs.

The knife of choice for Pyrenees shepherds

The rustic knife par excellence, the Capuchin seduced the whole of the countryside.

The extremely simple rustic knife, in the tradition of the primitive knife, was for a long time the most popular folding model among country folk, even after the appearance of the spring, which revolutionized the design of clasp knives. Regional varieties included the Jambette, the Dauphine, the Foyard and the Montpellier, each with an individual shape. The Capuchin was the typical knife of the Pyrenees shepherd.

Its design? A wide willow-leaf blade, a one-piece handle in yellow horn. The blade was fixed to the handle with a nail, on which it swiveled freely, folding into the slit sawn into the handle for the purpose. When opened, the heel of the blade was stopped by another nail placed slightly above the axis, preventing the horn of the handle from damage. Naturally, due to the lack of a spring, the blade was not held firmly in an open position and, with wear and loosening of parts, the movement became too fluid, necessitating a couple of good hammer blows to knock the nails back into position and tighten up the mechanism.

Since mediaeval times, this simple, rustic knife was frequently found in the Southwest of France, up until the Second World War when it fell out of use, their owners preferring to switch to spring-loaded models that were more reliable, and safer. Ever since 1960 there have been occasional attempts to reintroduce it, but it has only been with the relatively recent vogue of regionalism that it has gained a following among those nostalgic for a bygone age.

But why the name Capuchin? Quite simply because the handle, with the blade folded into it, resembles the profile of a monk, their head covered by a cowl. Moreover, shepherds, who tend to be quite handy with a knife, very often carved the handle so that the monk's head stood out clearer. This gave the Cognet company the idea of bringing out a luxurious model of this traditional knife, with a beautifully carved monk's head on the handle.

In the mountains of the Pyrenees, no one would ever have dreamed of cutting their ewe's cheese with any other knife!

It was a frequent practice for shepherds to sculpt the handle so that the Capuchin stood out.

Popular, effective and recognizable

In the 15th century it started to become common practice to decorate the handles of folding knives, with techniques varying according to the materials used. Ivory and wood were carved, silver and copper engraved, while bone and porcelain were painted. Certain bronze or copper handles were molded or stamped. This principle was used by a certain Léon Coursolle at the beginning of the 20th century, and this knife soon passed into posterity, first of all in Western France and then throughout the country; it is still as much appreciated today.

Léon's Coursolle's design was original: to fit the mechanism between two brass plaques that served as both holding plates and sides. This economized on materials and saved on assembly time. But the appearance was rather too austere, and so the idea of engraving the handle was resurrected. The services of Mr. Okinsburger were called upon, a celebrated engraver at the Paris Mint, who had exercised his art on the molds used for stamping. All Léon Coursolle had to do was to dust off his old trade of peddler and go

Multi-bladed, simple and robust, it still has its essential elements.

round the country drumming up interest in the object.

The range soon diversified, as much in the subjects that decorated the blades— pretty lady, hunter, basketball player, various animals, etc.—as in the sizes and blades: single, double, corkscrew, can opener, awl, etc.

Of course the new cutlery arrival had to be identified, and this was done by registering the trademark in 1920, the logo of which was no more nor less than a spanner, or rather four spanners of different sizes on which the Coursolle name was added.

The Coursolle knife is today produced by Coupérier in Thiers, the town where it was born a century ago…

There are numerous motifs for every taste.

Wreathed in symbolism and mystery

It might seem surprising to mention secrecy in connection with knives. It does not refer to a secret technique for manufacturing them, but rather a mechanism requiring knowledge of its quite particular operation in order to release it, that is to say open or close it. Or else the knife could simply be a pretext, that is to say it looks like a knife but is in fact a secret box where one might hide a jewel, a deadly pill… or any other object that its owner might wish to keep safe from prying eyes…or hands… It was naturally essential that no curious person be able to open this apparent knife, which was why it had a secret mechanism.

We should not forget that the heyday of these objects was in the 17th and 18th centuries, a time of high intrigues where it was safer to trust no one, which explains why so many pieces of furniture, particularly writing desks, were designed with hidden drawers or secret opening mechanisms. Moreover, symbolism was much in evidence in a multitude of areas, understood by a handful of initiates, whether scientists, alchemists or Grand Masters of secret societies.

In his monumental work of 1771, *The Cutler's Craft,* Jean-Jacques Perret devotes a whole chapter to "knives with various secrets," illustrated with numerous plates, and giving advice and tips concerning their manufacture. Some of these knives carried nicknames: "military knife," "fly knife," "broken spring knife" and even "grimace knife!"

A secret knife, full of mystery…

The model shown here, exhibited in the Thiers Cutlery Museum, is the secret knife par excellence. It dates from the end of the 17th century. Only its owner would be able to open it since it uses a code…the mechanism being released by placing the planet and clock-hand in the right positions. Its symbolism (planet, star, etc.) is as mysterious as the nature of its owner—alchemist, astronomer, Grand Master or loyal servant?

Symbol of the Celts and Merlin the Enchanter?

*A reproduction
Celtic knife
to which the young
cutler Ludovic Marsile
has added his personal touch,
a trefoil and an ermine.*

I s there any other region of France so steeped in mystery and legend as is Brittany? Lines of standing stones, whose symbolism still escapes us, Cromlechs, dolmens, tumuli, cairns and all those other megalithic monuments that were erected or built between 5,000 and 2,000 B.C., vestiges of a mystical tradition…

But the Celtic influence in Brittany is also considerable, with legends of the Round Table, King Arthur and his quest for the Grail, and Merlin the Enchanter in the Forest of Brocéliande. The Celts arrived on this peninsula, that they named "Armor," in the 6th century B.C. Kicked out by Ceasar, they returned in the year 460 and left an indelible trace that has profoundly influenced the whole of the Breton culture. However, while Brittany is the land of magicians, fairies and diverse beliefs and practices, it is also the land of saints, who can be counted in the hundreds. Religion is thus omnipresent, with each church or cathedral having its own patron saint.

In this land swept by sea spray, a knife is a most useful implement. The regional model, produced in Thiers in the 19th century, was called the "London," but its recent descendant is called "Gwalarn," which sounds better. A very popular mariners' knife, it has been considered the regional knife ever since it was born, with its rounded handle and shape of blade that immediately stands out.

But there is another, older, less well-known model, typically Celtic, since it was found during digs of archaeological sites dating from 800 B.C., which would make it one of the oldest known folding knives. Small, with a half-moon blade that swivels on an axis to fold into a bone handle engraved with a solar symbol, it is preserved in Rennes.

Ludovic Marsille, a young bladesmith who set up his forge in the depths of the Forest of Brocéliande, has scrupulously reproduced it, adding a little personal touch in the form of a trefoil at the end of the handle.

It is perhaps the ancestor of the Breton knife with which the fairies cut the plants they required for their magic potions. There also exist other knives, slimmer and larger for tougher jobs, also produced exquisitely by the younger generation of local bladesmiths.

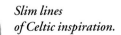

*Slim lines
of Celtic inspiration.*

A blade which swivels on an axis, folding into its horn sheath that serves as a handle.

Five thousand years of tradition

How can one not be surprised, when visiting the museums of Aléria, Levie or Sartène, to learn that Corsican knifemaking is five thousand years old… The island took advantage of its mineral sites very early on in its history to produce metals: four thousand years ago for copper, and around the 6th century B.C. for iron. During this long history, we of course find military knives, from the dagger that appears carved on standing stones at various sites to the famous stilettos of the Corsican army in the 18th century. The most typical knives, however, are the utilitarian models. The major activities on the island are agriculture and livestock. So shepherds, herdsmen, farmers and basket-makers use a knife daily, both at work and at home

Whether the "Spuntichu," "Curnachjola," "Runchetta," "Temperinu," "Cultella pittuda," or regional knives like those from Ascu or Niolu, there is no shortage of different models. After a long period of neglect, the traditional knife was reintroduced in 1975 by Paul Santoni,

Christian Moretti rekindled the Corsican forges to make damascene using locally extracted minerals.

based on an ancient model called the "Temperinu." Under the aegis of Christian Moretti, a Metallurgical Ethnography and Research Center was established in Lumio, which enabled blades to be forged using traditional methods and minerals extracted from Corsican soil.

The "cursina," the Corsican knife par excellence, found itself once more in production, with its characteristic forged blade, strong, rounded and swiveling on an axis to fold into its horn handle. Due to the lack of a spring or mechanism the blade can never be kept securely open so it is gripped between one's fingers, with the handle really serving as no more than a sheath. There are two notches on the reverse of the blade which are the modern replacement of the tool used by joiners and carpenters in times past to make notches in wood. We should not forget that until not so long ago, wooden utensils were used in the country kitchen: forks, spoons and plates. This knife was thus also intended for working and decorating wood in the craft tradition.

It finally reappears
hardly modernized at all

A regional knife may be both very simple and yet extremely beautiful, like this Sauveterre, also called the "Wine Merchant."

There are many people who, even in town, still carry a folding knife in their pocket that they use on numerous occasions. Not so long ago, everyone in the countryside had his own knife from which he would not be separated for anything in the world. Today's city-dweller perhaps reproduces unconsciously the behavior of his father or grandfather.

These are regional models, in the sense that every region once had its own that was quite distinct and characteristic, even bearing a name for better identification.

The Alpin in the Alps and Savoie; the Massu (club) in Alsace; the Mineur in the North; the London in Brittany; the Navette (shuttle) in Paris; the Donjon (castle keep) in Bresse; the Berger (shepherd) in the Pyrenees; the Férréol in Poitou-Charentes; the Queue de Poisson (fish-tail) in the Vendée; the Piétain in Champagne; the Tonneau (barrel) in the Berry; the Tiré droit (straight draw) in the Morvan; the Gouttière (gutter) in the Jura, etc. Of course many others simply bore the name of their region or of a local town: the Aurillac, the Yssingeaux, the Aveyronnais, the Sauveterre; the Langres. Then there is the most famous of all, the Laguiole, or the very ancient Nontron… Here and there one could find a model that bore the name of its

brand, the Pradel for example, and that no one had dared rename.

These folding regional knives had a single blade, or perhaps two, with accessories according to local needs. Does this mean then that the knives were manufactured in the regions concerned, or that their shape resulted from local traditions? Surprisingly, even disappointingly, the answer is categorically no! In fact, if we take the two most famous knives, we discover that the Laguiole is of Spanish inspiration and that the Nontron was of Moorish influence. As for the others, that is to say all those that we have just mentioned, they were not produced in their region, except for a few, like the Sauvetterre, a long time before its wide commercialization! In fact, these regional knives appeared in the second half of the 19th century, a time when nearly all cutlery production came from Thiers.

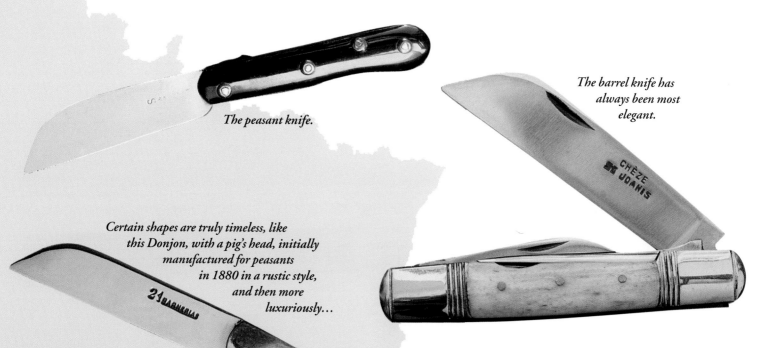

The peasant knife.

The barrel knife has always been most elegant.

Certain shapes are truly timeless, like this Donjon, with a pig's head, initially manufactured for peasants in 1880 in a rustic style, and then more luxuriously...

The reason why Thiers was able to hold onto its position, contrary to other areas which progressively stopped production, was due to its quite particular way of sharing out work, as well as an up-to-date production in very large quantities, helped by a buoyant market.

Producing is one thing, selling is another, particularly at a time when marketing methods were fairly rudimentary and the only way to get a product known was to hawk it around. So the representatives of these manufacturers would wind their way across France with the complete range in their suitcases. The models were proposed to retailers who then made their choice, either according to personal taste, or else because of a certain resemblance to a type of knife that existed in the region a long time ago, or even simply according to whatever was left in the suitcases. Sometimes the model was given a name which suited the region well and would thus be a strong selling point. Otherwise they would be given the name of whatever place they were put on sale, since at this time knives were sold at fairs held in the principal town of a region, which is how we end up with Yssingeaux, Sauveterre, Aurillac, etc.

If ever they were asked to reproduce an existing model or to change a detail on one of their own models, adding an extra piece for example, nothing was simpler for the Thiers cutlers!

At any rate, these regional knives gave much satisfaction to several generations, and it is easy to understand why people today wish to reestablish a link with the past by slipping into their pocket the same knife that grandpa carried, which is now possible since most of these regional knives have been reproduced.

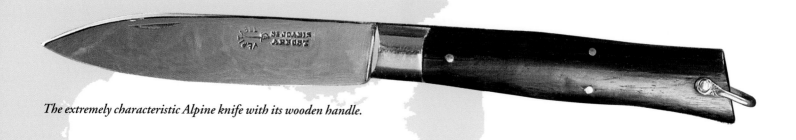

The extremely characteristic Alpine knife with its wooden handle.

A symbol of sharing

"Friend's knife," a surprising term at first, but if one remembers that table knives only appeared around the 11th and 12th centuries, and the fork even later (15th century), then one understands a little better.

In fact, the straight knife, worn at the belt, has always been an inseparable companion of man, who used it for all daily tasks, including eating.

The first table knives were pointed, enabling them to carve meat, then stab the morsel and carry it to the mouth. The end only became rounded quite late, after use of the fork had become widespread, having previously been used only at court. So at a time when the table knife did not yet exist, it was prudent to have one's own at mealtimes, particularly if invited to dine; otherwise there was a risk of being confronted with a serious problem, since in these distant times a knife was a deeply personal object, just like a toothbrush might be today. In addition, it was quite rare, in any given house, for there to be more than one per member of the family.

Naturally, it was only among the bourgeoisie and aristocracy that such embarrassing problems might arise, for rural folk and the common people always had a knife with them, since they were obliged to use it daily.

So a talented cutler had the idea for a friend's knife, conceived in a particularly ingenious way.

It consists of two folding knives, completely identical, held together by two rivets, but which can be split into two separate knives, enabling one to be lent to a friend who has forgotten his.

Considering the kind of people for whom they were intended, these knives were of course beautifully manufactured, with a handle in tortoise shell, ivory or mother-of-pearl.

Easy to take apart, with one half for its owner and the other for a friend.

A perfect finish

*A shuttle-shaped handle
and switchblade mechanism with ring
are typical of Nogent production.*

S ituated right in the middle of the Haute-Marne, equidistant from Langres and Chaumont, this little town is known all over the world for its cutlery industry, which has been established there since the 18th century. At that time there were no less than six thousand cutlers in Nogent, outpacing Langres and even causing the latter's cutlery activity to come to a halt after three centuries. Nogent produced mainly small cutlery, manicure instruments and scissors, but when it received an order in 1793 for fifteen thousand sabre blades, followed by an order from the Convention in 1795 for an impressive quantity of bayonets, the Société Populaire de Nogent proved itself capable of delivering on time.

The production of Nogent was quite similar to that of Paris in style and genre, exported well, and was exhibited, notably in London, where in 1851 Mr. de Hennezel, spokesman for the exhibition jury, declared: "Nogent produces different kinds of fine, semi-fine and ordinary cutlery items; its fine scissors and pocket knives are the most beautifully manufactured in the whole Universe!"

The Nogent cutlery industry was also highlighted at the Universal Exhibition in 1855 and at many others. Nogent thus stands for fine cutlery par

excellence, some objects so beautifully crafted that they are true works of art.

Today, a few names are still cherished among collectors: Vitry, for example, for its excellent and highly reputed manicure accessories; Eloi Pernet, who excel in the art of the penknife and nail scissors, produced in a variety of styles, but always perfect. The typical Nogent knife is either a single-bladed folding model, with a "shuttle" handle in horn, and a switchblade mechanism activated by a ring placed on the external spring, or else a multi-bladed folding knife, without a switchblade mechanism of the "Swiss Army Knife" type, but beautifully crafted down to the smallest details and decorated with luxurious plaques of horn or ivory.

*The Nogent knife has
always been luxuriously
crafted.*

Everywhere, even in the most unexpected places

Identifiable among
thousands, with
its red handle
bearing the Swiss
escutcheon.

A small white cross on the red handle of a folding knife, such is the trademark that enables one to identify a Swiss Army Knife at a glance. The incredible story begins with Karl Elsener, who was born in 1860. Having learned the cutler's craft in Zug, the town of his forefathers, he opened his own workshop in 1884 in Ibach and immediately showed his sharpened sense of marketing, getting himself known through a series of advertisements published in local papers, and by placing some of his knives in various clothing accessory shops, including his father's hat shop. In 1891, he founded the Swiss Cutlery Guild, whose main objective was to be able, by combined effort, to do something that no one had yet been able to achieve on their own, that is to manufacture the pocket knife for the army of the Swiss Confederation. Up until then, the Swiss military had ordered its knives from Solingen, the center of German knifemaking.

The first delivery of these new knives was made in October 1891, consisting of a model called the "Soldier's Knife," weighing 144 grams, with wooden plaques for the handle, a single blade, awl, can opener and screwdriver.

But although very robust, it was rather heavy, so an "officer's" model was designed and officially registered on June 12, 1897. Despite two additional pieces (a second, smaller blade and a corkscrew), this model was lighter and much more elegant; as for the plaques, they were made from red fiber. Immediately adopted by the army, great interest was also shown in these models by a civilian clientele, inside Switzerland at first, and then far beyond its borders. Over the years these two models have undergone various evolutions. The "soldier," for example, was made twenty grams lighter in 1908, with the wooden sides, whose main defect was that they fissured too quickly, replaced by others made from fiber. In 1951, 35 grams were again saved by using stainless steel. In 1961, red alox was used for the sides, and the weight dropped still further to 72 grams! In 1965, it was trimmed with silver alox, and in 1980 the Swiss escutcheon was placed on it. As for the "officer" model, this escutcheon was placed on it in 1909, in 1936 the fiber was replaced by Celluloid, in 1946 the can opener was improved, in 1951 alox was used for the separators,

Karl Elsener, founder of the dynasty.

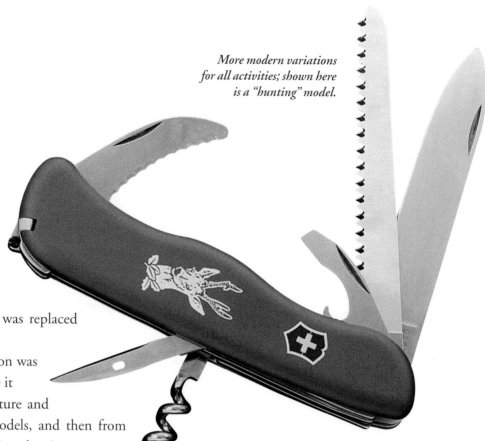

More modern variations for all activities; shown here is a "hunting" model.

and in 1968 the initial attachment was replaced by a ring.

The reason why a Swiss blazon was placed on it in 1909 was to designate it clearly as an item of Swiss manufacture and thus distinguish it from German models, and then from imitations, since it goes without saying that in any era a good product can only be copied. It was necessary to identify it better though, and thus protect it, using a commercial name. In 1909, Karl Elsener's mother died, and he decided to use her first name, Victoria, for the brand. The firm's founder worked himself relentlessly, perhaps even to death, departing this world at the age of fifty-eight; he was succeeded by his sons, Carl and Alois. In 1921, stainless steel made its appearance under the name "Inox" and this was added to the brand, which, when contracted, became "Victorinox."

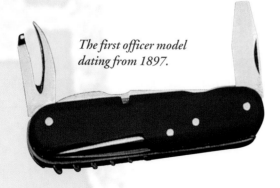

The first officer model dating from 1897.

But orders, both civil and military, had been so huge since the establishment of the company that Karl Elsener had never been able to fully satisfy the demand. That was why another company was created in Switzerland in 1906, under the name Wenger, which also made Swiss Army Knives for soldiers, officers and civilians with the same red sides and the same white cross, but placed at the center of a square with rounded edges. The two companies have worked together ever since, with each one developing an infinite range of models so that the tools in these little knives will respond to all needs.

From the slim four-piece "Soldier's Knife" to the imposing twenty-one piece "Toolkit," who would dare to claim that they couldn't find what they were seeking? A special model for hunters with a switchblade mechanism, another for anglers, yet others for horse riders, golfers, campers, sailors, skippers, and even a "Special Fireman" model!

The conquest of Africa

A handle in folded sheet-metal and a blade in very good steel, here is the Douk-Douk in all its simplicity.

At the start of the last century, Antoine Cognet became the head of the firm Soanen-Mondanel, a cutler in Thiers, which had been manufacturing folding knives that had been developed in 1835 by *La Coutellerie Française*, whose blades were stamped with a hare. Gaspard Cognet, who curiously enough everyone called Gaston, succeeded his father, but was soon faced with major difficulties, the French economy being in a somewhat shaky state after the First World War. In addition, exports, which had been a major source of revenue, had crumbled, and so it was vital to find new markets.

That was how Gaston had the idea, in 1929, of designing a good quality folding knife for daily use at an affordable price. It was a very flat knife, the handle of which was simply a piece of folded sheet metal, onto which was fixed a blade swiveling on an axis and held by a spring. It was essential that this blade be forged from the best steel and that its cutting edge be tough enough to handle anything. Once the knife had been produced, all that remained was to find a country to export it to. Which one did they choose? Melanesia!

Why did they choose this collection of Pacific Islands? Because it was far away, unknown and totally free from commercial invasion! Gaston, who was neither short of audacity nor of imagination, set about looking for a name that would favor the sale of his new baby. He researched this far-off country with its strange beliefs, and his attention was grabbed by a picture decorating the cover of an old book: a character covered in feathers, wearing a pointed hat and with bare legs. His name? Douk-Douk! Such an original name, pronounceable in all languages, and such an unusual silhouette would clearly stand out. The idea was received with enthusiasm!

However, perhaps he should have gone a little further in his research concerning the significance of this figure, since Douk-Douk embodies the spirit of punishment for the Melanesians and plays the role of scaring those who have something to fear or to hide… The brand was registered in 1930 and production started on a grand scale, but the attempt to conquer these distant South Sea islands met with total failure. It was never clear if this

*It is even possible
to decorate the handle
in different ways…*

*An old catalog displaying
a wide variety of symbols.*

was due to the unfortunate choice of symbol, but Gaston Cognet was not a man to be shaken by such setbacks, and he soon set sail for another destination, North Africa.

This time, the knife found immediate success, with 98 percent of production being exported. After trying their hand in North Africa, why shouldn't they try heading south, before turning their attentions to Lebanon, or Indochina? Everywhere it went the knife was received with greater appreciation than they dared hope, but the reasons for this success had little to do with luck. In fact, the quality of the cutting edge was remarkable, with the blade made from fine carbon steel, forged in special ovens burning hardwood charcoal, followed by a special tempering process in the workshop. In addition, so that each country would have its own connection with the knife, the original effigy was replaced by others, including a lion, a fox and a Southern Cross, and the models named the "Tiki," the "El Baraka," the "Saharien," and the "Ed-Dib." The impact was such that, for certain people, the Douk-Douk became a currency.

To have had the idea of designing and producing such a knife during a lean economic period, simple, cheap, light, flat to the point that its owner would forget it was in their pocket, while ensuring an uncompromisingly high-quality blade and creating a whole legend surrounding it, really is a magnificent and amazing feat worthy of much admiration, particularly if one considers that it had been necessary to roam distant lands at a time when such places were conspicuous neither by their economy nor safety for Europeans!

The Douk-Douk now inspires the best bladesmiths, like Jean-Pierre Veysseyre for this model.

Two hundred years of good and loyal service

E ustache, Jambette and Capuchin all belong to the same family: knives swiveling on a nail without a spring and manufactured over a period of nearly two hundred years from the middle of the 17th century to the middle of the 19th century in the Saint-Etienne region. This explains why the Jambette, for example, is generally called the "Saint-Etienne Jambette." But if there is a knife that symbolizes perfectly the rural life, then it is certainly the Eustache, sold all over the country and beyond!

It owes its name to the Saint-Etienne knifemaker Eustache Dubois, who made it his specialty at the end of the 17th century. Fougeroux de Bondary, in his work entitled *The Art of the Cutler in Everyday Knives,* mentions that many of these knives were made elsewhere than in the Forez region, but nowhere in such great quantities: five to six hundred thousand in total! According to the Forez manufacturer, they had different names.

The Eustache, in a particularly elegant older version.

Around 1850, these knives were nothing but memories for the inhabitants of Saint-Etienne… However, since there was still a nostalgic desire for them, they were eventually manufactured once more by the Thiers knifemakers.

The example photographed, which is exhibited at the Thiers Cutlery Museum, is entirely representative of the design, as well as being precisely dated.

The names of its owner, Gabriel du Naud, and the person who gave it to him, Jean Delaise, are both engraved on the handle along with the date, 1739. The handle is made from boxwood and the blade has a turned-down point. Its particularity is the long collar that sheaths part of the handle. Nostalgic knife collectors might be interested to know that a copy has been recently produced that is faithful down to the smallest detail, particularly in the luxury model.

The oldest popular knife in France

Cutlery centers were thick on the ground in France a few centuries ago, and if there was a particularly well-known one then it was Nontron, a large village in the Dordogne where the living was good, with truffles, foie gras and conserves also adding to the region's renown. It is said that in the 15th century Paris cutlers made their way there, not only to get a good meal, but also to pick up a few tricks of the trade from the local craftsmen.

So Nontron gave its name to a knife, as did Laguiole, and here we have one of the oldest popular knives in France. In spite of existing in different versions this knife clearly stands out from all others. Its handle is made from boxwood, a robust wood in warm tones, which ages well. But it is characterized by two other elements. Firstly, its shape, the end of which may be "boule," "carp-tailed," "clog" and even "violin." There is also a poker-work decoration, a "V" surrounded by three points that the locals call a "mouche" (fly). A collar keeps the blade firmly open, which is usually "willow-leaf," or sometimes "Catalan" in shape.

A rural knife, regional, rustic, popular and particularly old, it has been part of the local heritage for five cen-turies. Still manufactured by hand, it is just as popular today. Why such an original, timeless and unusual style? History does not say. As for the legend, it suggests Moorish inspiration (Poitiers, where the Moors were finally defeated in 732 after ravaging Provence and the Rhône valley, is not that far away) but that is only the legend.

At any rate, in this Dordogne where it was born, there would be no question of "making" a slice of foie gras with a knife that was not integral to local customs, and there are rumors that more than one goose or duck owes their dispatch to the next world to it.

But maybe that is only evil tongues wagging…

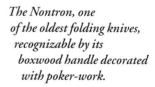

The Nontron, one of the oldest folding knives, recognizable by its boxwood handle decorated with poker-work.

Heritage, history and legend

A very old Calmels Laguiole with an ivory handle.

The Laguiole? More than a knife, it is a pinch of Aubrac earth and a sign of recognition for those Auvergne folk who left for Paris! Some villages have a history, others a legend. For having given its name to this famous knife, Laguiole, a small Aubrac village, has both. Under the Ancien Régime, the only knife production center in the Rouergue was at Sauveterre. In 1850, only four craftsmen were making rustic knives in Laguiole inspired by Sauveterre, that is to say one-piece folding knives with a "willow-leaf" blade, a miter and, of course, a "mouche" (fly), which is the piece of metal that enables the heel of the blade to stop against the spring. Whether a simple piece of metal or one decorated as a "fly," this part is always called a "mouche."

These four cutlers were named Pagès, Glaize, Mas and Pierre-Jean Calmels, who was the first to set up his forge in the village and who remained working alone there for many years; it is thus his name that has gone down to posterity.

He excelled in the manufacture of remarkable knives, and in 1829 produced a model that he called "the Laguiole," although it was quite different from those that we now know. Calmels was thus unanimously acclaimed as the creator of the Laguiole.

His inspiration? It was certainly not from the "capuchadou," as has often been erroneously written, since that is a straight knife of extremely simple design used for centuries by all and sundry before the folding knife developed and became universally popular. The Laguiole was a successor to the "capuchadou" that it soon replaced definitively.

The Calmels knife did, in any case, immediately attract the local clientele by its practicality and completely new design. The blade was shaped like a yataghan (curved Muslim knife), totally inspired from the Spanish navaja, and the handle was curved like that of the Jambette de Saint-Etienne, known since the 18th century, and two brass miters were placed on the handle, exactly like the stöika, a knife from Eastern-Europe. This mix of styles produced a completely original knife, however, one which has evolved with time, since in 1840 an awl was added so that herdsmen could pierce the belly of a cow suffering from a build-up of gas. In 1880 a corkscrew was added, an essential tool for the

*A "full-handle" enables very
beautiful carving to be undertaken.*

*Handle-design provides
an infinite source of inspiration.*

numerous Aubrac folk who had moved to Paris, where many of them had become café owners.

The handle was generally made from horn, a material that was not in short supply in a region where there were many herds of cattle. However, much more luxurious models existed in ivory, sometimes sculpted in a completely original way. Such models, like those designed by such artists as Crocombette, to cite the most famous one, are now museum pieces. Fortunately the young village craftsmen of today are able to reproduce some of them. But a Laguiole is not just a knife, but a whole legend. There are many intriguing details, starting with the notches that decorate the back of the blade, sometimes seven in all. A reminder of the seven deadly sins perhaps?

Then there is the guillochage (engraving of patterns using fine lines) on the spring, executed from back to front: does this signify that one must always follow a path in order to evolve, or does it represent the water of a river that keeps on flowing whatever we do, as does time? Then there is the studding on the handle, in the shape of a cross contained in a shuttle. Christ's Cross before which the shepherd prostrates himself, and the lozenge, traced in tiny studs, a rosary? Finally the "mouche," which becomes a bee… A nod to the large number of

them in the region, or else a homage to Napoleon, who chose the bee to replace the lily on the royal coat of arms?

Yes, the Laguiole legend certainly makes it much more than simply a knife; that must have surely been the source of its charm and its success for such a long time and no doubt for many years to come.

*Certain
craftsmen, like Angel
Navarro, added a real
Hispanic touch to their knives.*

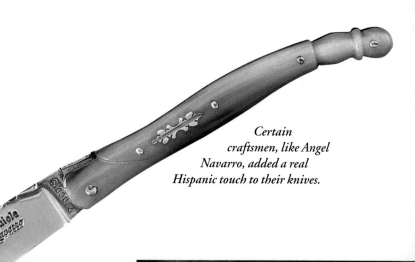

*The appearance
of the corkscrew changed
the aesthetic of handles.*

The knife that became a work of art

S lim and elegant, the Laguiole is a knife that many artists immediately wished to exercise their talent on. Nicolas Crocombette is certainly the most well-known, he who raised this simple rural knife to the level of a work of art in its own right.

Born in Thiers, the young Nicolas was set to become a notary's clerk, but his family encountered financial difficulties and so had to give it up. Of weak constitution, suffering respiratory and vertebral problems, he was obliged to find an activity that did not require physical effort, but all that did not prevent him from living to a ripe old age: born in 1863 he died in 1955! He was drawn toward activities requiring artistic skills: engraving, chiseling and sculpture, on steel first of all and then on ivory. He started off working in the Thérias cutlery, where he soon acquired unbelievable renown.

He devoted himself almost entirely to the Laguiole, to which he brought many details that would later become an integral part of the knife—the engraving on the spring, first of all, and even chiseling, which was then copied by other cutlers in simple guillochage. Then came the "mouche," which was sometimes just a flat piece of metal, for which Crocombette had the idea of a multitude of motifs: a clover, an animal, an acorn, and many others… Finally the ivory han-

dle, which he sculpted admirably and in a totally personal way, including the body of a woman carved from the whole handle, something that also required the plates to be hewn to shape.

Some of his designs can be admired in the Laguiole museum, as well as the Cutlery Museum in Thiers. When the Thiers municipality decided to present a gift to President Lebrun, it gave him a "Crocombette," which earned the artist the Legion of Honor!

A model that is characteristic of the Crocombette style, and perhaps the most famous.

Was this artist also responsible for this type of "full-handle?" At any rate, his models were some of the most successful.

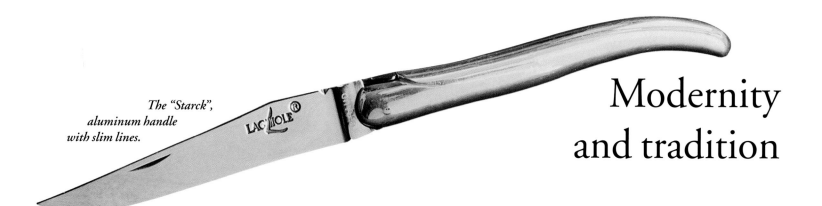

*The "Starck",
aluminum handle
with slim lines.*

Modernity
and tradition

There is no doubt about the renown of Laguiole. However, France experienced a period of economic difficulty not so long ago that affected a number of industries, the cutlery industry in particular. In addition, fashions come and go, and this knife was no exception, lying forgotten after the war until about 1983. In the village itself, between 1930 and 1985 practically the only knifemaker at work was Calmels. The municipality acted, however, to blow life back into the ashes of this famous knife that lay at the origin of the site's reputation. From 1985, shops slowly started to establish themselves and the village became the place to buy a Laguiole, even though it was now completely manufactured in Thiers.

In 1987, a factory with a futuristic shape, conceived by the famous designer Philippe Starck, was built, and the various parts were produced and assembled there. Several models were created, including one designed by the talented Starck, which had the particularity of having an aluminum handle. Of course this concept had already existed for a long time, a similar model having been registered at the beginning of the century by a Thiers knifemaker, but the merit lay once more in turning to this metal that lent itself well to slim shapes. Calling on a personal-

ity known all over the world also enabled a new image of this knife to be created, bringing it up to date.

Other local cutlers preferred to carry on the tradition, like Honoré Durand, who set up a forge to produce the best possible blades and who, in his Coutellerie de Laguiole, gets young artists to carve "Crocombette" models executed with close regard to the tiniest detail.

Whether in continuity or modernity, the Laguiole, now entirely manufactured in its place of origin, has obviously not stopped inspiring new talent!

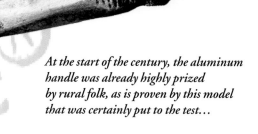

*At the start of the century, the aluminum
handle was already highly prized
by rural folk, as is proven by this model
that was certainly put to the test…*

From the simple nail file to the portable manicure kit

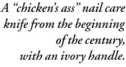

A "chicken's ass" nail care knife from the beginning of the century, with an ivory handle.

Eloi Pernet had the ingenuity of fitting the two blades in an original way.

The penknife was first of all intended for sharpening a quill pen, scratching off dried ink and opening letters, but from the moment when it became possible to fit two blades in a folding knife, there was nothing to stop even more being fitted, and for completely different uses. The small, flat penknife was the preserve of wealthier people, and was thus a beautiful and luxurious object, designed to be useful and easily carried, whether in a pocket for men or a handbag for women.

So that is how the principle of two opposing blades was kept: the little blade remained to sharpen goose quills, with the second replaced by a nail file. The first manicure kit was thus born, before being improved upon in various ways. Since a larger and sturdier blade than that used for sharpening quills appeared necessary, three-piece kits appeared, the third piece being the required larger and

From the simple "penknife/nail care tool" the next step was a complete miniature manicure-kit.

sturdier blade for cutting more resistant material. The resulting "cul-de-poule" (literally: chicken's ass) model remained in vogue for a long time, with the idea of putting the file flat on the back of the knife enabling a more discreet object to be made.

But development could not stop there, for the beautiful ladies, used to kits brimming over with accessories, would not be satisfied with this standby kit. The cutlers of Paris and Nogent thus set to making real folding and portable manicure kits consisting of a file, cuticle remover, nail cleaner, scissors, blades, and even sometimes a small polisher.

Since the penknife shape did not lend itself to such a set, other, more compact shapes were found, and it is certainly to Eloi Pernet, of Nogent, that we owe the most beautiful pieces, some of which are still manufactured today.

ELOI PERNET

The French cutlery capital finally gets a knife all of its own

Remarkable damascene work, with Pirou castle, dear to the Thiernois, shown on the handle.

As surprising as it may appear, Thiers, which can rightly claim to be the French cutlery capital and which for five centuries has been making knives intended for all the regions of France, did not have its "own" knife! The name of the town was never actually mentioned, with the models taking the names of the families who made them, or the names of the places or activities for which they were intended: Pradel, Coursolle, Yssingeaux, Aurillac, the Alpin, the Mineur, the London, and of course the Laguiole, made exclusively here for nearly a century!

The man responsible for it all was Jean-Pierre Treille, a living encyclopaedia and passionate enthusiast of the Thiers cutlery industry. He persuaded a group of knifemaker friends to join him in creating a representative model, knowing that since there would be neither history nor legend attached to it then they would have to invent these by delving into tradition. The principle of a brotherhood was adopted, with a Grand Master at the head of it. The knife model envisioned had to have a line that was evocative of the region, to characterize the height of local know-how without being too marked by what had already been produced. The shape should thus be both traditional and innovative so as to ensure the transition between the past to which the town owed so much and the third millenium. The approved prototype conformed to the required conditions, being representative of the region, with a character of its own and an original design. Only a folding model could naturally meet this challenge.

There simply remained to find a name: "couté de Tié" was chosen, which means "Thiers knife" in the local patois. As for the logo, this was a capital "T" followed by a dot, placed in a square.

In 1994, the country now boasted a new knife, the "Thiers," that each member of the brotherhood could produce in their own version according to a precise set of parameters and a quality charter. Thiers now possessed its "own" knife!

A magnificent version of the Thiers knife with a "secret" switchblade mechanism.

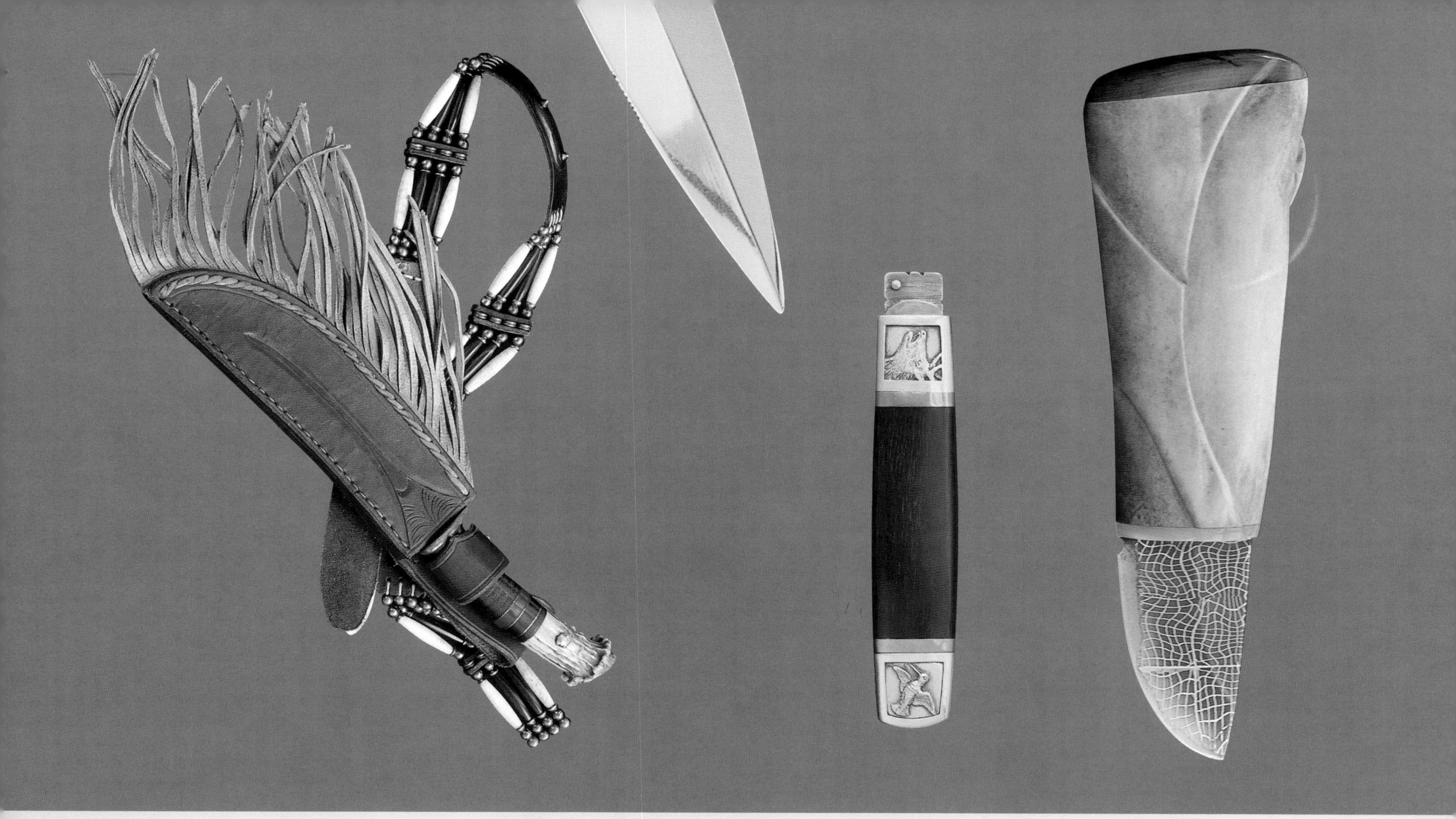

Specific knives

The knife that can handle any skin…

There is one thing that the Book of Genesis and Darwin both agree on: man was born naked and soon realized the need to clothe himself, not only to hide certain organs of which he had become aware, but also to replace his hairy coating that had been gradually thinning out as he evolved away from his primate ancestors. There was nothing quite as similar to a furry coat than…well…another furry coat! So it was logical that man turned toward animals that had not undergone the same evolutionary process and which had remained furry. Pelts are consumed neither by hominids nor other predators, and it is clear that those with which our ancestors clothed themselves were taken from dead prey encountered by chance. Apart from the fact that only skins without a single ounce of flesh left could be used, these pelts must have been atrociously stiff, since tanning techniques had not yet appeared.

As he became more skilled, man learned to "fashion" any skins he found by using flint scrapers. With the development of hunting came the necessity to actually remove the meat without damaging the precious skin, which was separated from the flesh with the aid of a sharp fragment of flint like a razor—the first "skinner" in a long line.

Such is the name for the type of knife intended exclusively for skinning furry animals. The first ones were simply chance implements, but as time went by the specialists of the time naturally developed shapes that were the best suited to such meticulous but rapid work. Although the skinner has appeared in many different forms throughout the ages and in various places, often very personalized, there is no doubt that it is to the Inuit whom we owe the most original shape—a half-moon—one that is as old as time. As for the

An elegant semi-skinner.

*The skinner
in its purest form.*

rest, it is in North America that this genre has known the largest number of variants. Considering the abundance of furry animals on this continent it was inevitable that a particular category of men would devote themselves to hunting them. These men were trappers and they rivaled each other in their ingenuity. A wide choice presented itself to them: bison, bear, deer, elk, marmot, raccoon, beaver, wolf, fox, lynx and otter...

The size of the knife thus depends on the size of the animal, but the choice is truly infinite as regards shape. The operation actually consists of removing the skin in a single piece without accidentally piercing it, which would considerably reduce its value, and cutting so as to leave as little flesh and fat on the pelt as possible. The blade thus needs to be as wide as can be so that it forms the ideal and constant

*A very rounded point
prevents the skin
from being pierced.*

angle, when placed on the body of the animal, required to successfully complete the operation. In addition, the point is clearly upturned and often rounded so as to make it as non-aggressive as possible. The presence of a guard is not at all necessary, since no great effort is required. As for the handle, it takes the shapes and forms that suit the user best, according to his technique and hand.

These days, even if the numbers of bison that once roamed the great plains of the West are no longer what they once were before the construction of the railroad, and although the profession of trapper is no longer what it was, American hunters are still particularly attached to this practice of skinning, which explains why there is still a wide variety of skinners to offer, from models with small blades and handles for three-finger use to enormous "cake server" models, and a whole range in between, every taste is catered for.

The skinner is an integral part of the legend of the American pioneers.

For a traditional form of hunting, now mostly forgotten

Mention hunting and one usually thinks of hunting with a gun, with hounds or else lying in wait in a hide for the prey to cross one's path. However, there exist certain specific trapping practices, many of them closely linked to local or regional traditions, sometimes based in common law and long since enshrined in local customs. The means and methods of these forms of hunting are often scrupulously codified, with ancestral knowledge being transmitted orally. An example of this is the Decree of the 16th November 1992 made by the French Council of State conferring legal status on the trapping of thrushes, lapwings and plovers.

In the Ardennes, lapwings and plovers are captured using nets called "vagnolis"; thrushes, whether redwing, song thrush, fieldfare or mistlethrush are trapped on branches. In order to do this, a twig is first cut, called the "pliette," on to which incisions are made so as to be able to fix a net. To make these incisions, a knife with a particularly keen point is required. A bunch of rowan berries is placed at one end of the twig and a last incision is made just in front of this, enabling a snare consisting of hair from a horse's mane to be attached to the twig (the hair must come from a stallion, but never a mare…). The thrush lands on the twig perch and in order to reach the berries sticks its neck through the snare, which closes around its neck when the thrush attempts to fly away…

Not so long ago, every trapper had a forge in his garden, enabling him to fashion the specific blade he required. But since they have been all but swept away by the winds of modernism, Jean Tanazacq, a renowned local knifemaker, had the idea of assisting these hunters by producing a knife specifically for trapping, with a particularly keen point and fearsome cutting edge. So the good folk of the Ardennes can sleep quietly in their beds, safe in the knowledge that thrush trapping may continue for many a long year yet…

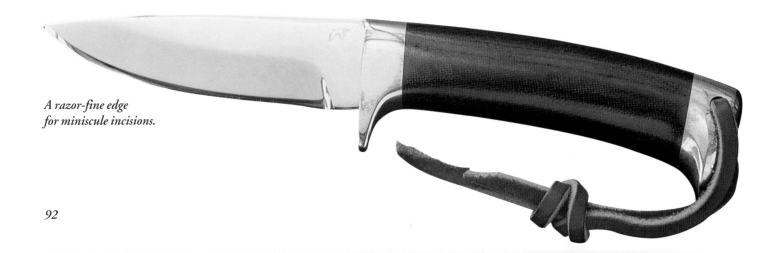

*A razor-fine edge
for miniscule incisions.*

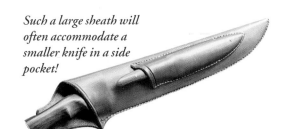

Such a large sheath will often accommodate a smaller knife in a side pocket!

A long knife that can handle anything

H unting is an adventure that often requires long journeys on foot or horseback, in Africa or the Canadian North for example. In these situations, you have to stop before night falls, bivouac and get a fire going, while during the daytime you sometimes have to set up a hide so as to watch without being seen… But you might also have to cut wood for a fire or hide while yet being relatively close to your home, perhaps in a nearby forest where you usually hunt and where you've built a little cabin to spend the night or eat a meal. The ideal instrument is undoubtedly the "camp knife," a long, slashing knife, straight out of the imagination of the great bladesmith Bill Moran, who knew masses about hunting and bivouacing right out in the middle of untamed nature.

Up until then the hatchet was the tool of choice, with a vast range of models available on the market, but it was heavy to wield and only used for chopping. The "camp knife," however, is capable of cutting, piercing and can even be used for skinning a large animal, for example, or even to defend oneself, which is not that unlikely an occurrence in these kinds of territories… But in order to be an attractive acquisition, though, it was necessary that its size and weight enable it to be worn at the belt without too much difficulty or fatigue. A "machete" type knife, for example, is rather cumbersome—its wearer certainly never forgets he's got it hanging from his belt!

If no one before Bill Moran had attempted such a perilous exercise, it was because it was inconceivable that the edge of such a thin blade, around 35 centimeters long, could resist successive strikes and yet still be able to cut. A extraordinary know-how was thus called for, that is to say a mastery of all of the subtleties of metallurgy, the forge and selective tempering. One can clearly understand why not only Bill Moran became a legend, but his "camp knife" too!

A sturdy "camp knife" with its protective sheath.

Obvious when you think about it

On some models the blade may be very short.

There are hundreds of names for knives, inspired perhaps by their creator (Opinel, Eustache, Coursolle, etc.), their origin (Bowie, D'Estaing, etc.), where they were first made (Laguiole, Nontron, etc.), their purpose (vet's knife, skinner, etc.), their mechanism (butterfly, liner lock, etc.) and, naturally, their brand (Buck, Kershaw, Puma, etc.), without forgetting the town or region with which they are associated (Sauveterre, Yssingeaux, Aurillac, etc.).

One might suppose that all possibilities had long since been explored and that there was not much left to invent, but that would be a rather reckless approach that would make light of the talent and imagination of certain knifemakers!

Bob Loveless is always on the lookout for a new shape, a detail that has hitherto escaped him, a material or a style. Despite his long experience and a renown that can only be envied, he was not satisfied with the shape of the points of his blades. He found them too rectilinear—a shape that had always been used in the United States. He had the idea of slightly lifting those of certain models, resulting in the "semi skinner," which was more polyvalent than the "traditional" skinner. He then designed a range of models with a cut-off point, resembling certain combat knives, for better penetration. This resulted in the "utility" knife par excellence. But our man was still not satisfied in his search for the "universal knife." He sat there mechanically opening and closing the blade of the Swiss Army Knife he held in his hand, until he suddenly got it: the solution was a blade of which the extremity swelled slightly, with a point that dropped, all of it rounded. He immediately started playing with his saw, and inspired by this principle that he then improved he produced the first "drop point" in the history of knifemaking! No one has yet bettered this design, which perhaps explains why it has been copied so much.

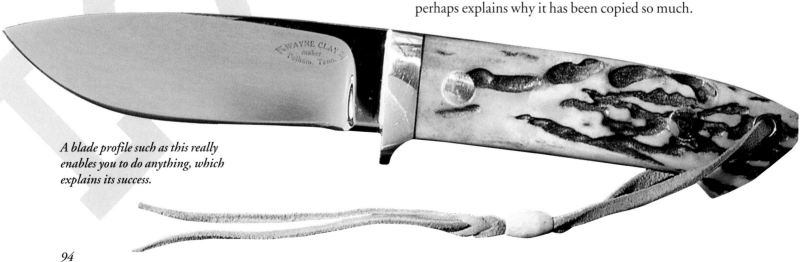

A blade profile such as this really enables you to do anything, which explains its success.

In memory of 1870

The Avenger of 1870.

The desire for vengeance may seem like a surprising feeling in a time of peace, but when the First World War broke out, the memory of the previous conflict against the same neighbor (the Franco-Prussian war of 1870) was all too present, with all of the stirred-up feelings one can imagine. In addition, there was a deep patriotism which never lacked an opportunity to display itself. That was how the "knife-dagger model 1916," as it was officially termed, became called "The Avenger of 1870." Indeed one of its manufacturers, Roddier & Dozolme, registered its own model on October 7, 1915 at the same time as another model, "the Revenge for 1870."

All the blademsiths who produced this model followed the patriotic vogue, as can be seen from the names of the fifty-odd brands registered, which run from the more sober, like the "Hairy," the "Knife of the Allies," the "Victorious," the "Conqueror," the "Patriot," the "Liberty Knife," the "Defender," the "Protector," and the "French Saviour," to mention but a few, to the more vindictive like the "Anti-Kraut," the "Death to the Krauts," or the "Anti-German." The impressive quantity of models produced in Thiers resulted in the amassing of such large stocks that this knife was also distributed in 1939-1940 to "trench-cleaning" sections, as well as to the irregular forces and tank crews. The official description of this dagger model 1916, according to archives of the period, is as follows: the extra-hard steel blade (often called sabre-blade steel) is rhombic in form and ends with a threaded tang; the guard and screw of the tang are in soft steel; the handle is in hard wood and the collar in half-hard steel; the sheath, in folded and brazed sheet-metal, is bronzed and bears, near to its opening, two longitudinal ribs on one side and a transversal rib on the other to hold the blade; the knife and sheath are both stamped with the distinctive letter of the supplier.

Belt sheath, made entirely from metal.

Every Thiers manufacturer stamped its own mark.

An American knife made in France

Model 1918, with bronze knuckle-duster handle.

I n December 1915, Georges Dubois, a Paris master of arms, proposed a most interesting dagger that he had just created to the minister of war of the time. The double-edged blade had a point of particular penetrative power, but its originality lay in the guard, a wraparound like that of a sabre and bearing pyramidal protuberances that served as a knuckle-duster. This model, with a turned-wood handle and leather sheath, was not accepted despite its superb design. However, our master of arms did not give up on his idea.

In fact, the United States officially adopted a model with a "knuckle-duster" handle called the "Trench Knife Model 1917." The blade was triangular in form and was thus not intended for cutting. It was mounted on a handle of oiled wood with a wraparound guard with six outward-facing pyramidal protuberances. A second version differed from the first in that the pyramids were no longer stamped but punched; in addition, there were only five of them and they were more like triangular teeth.

Since these models were not entirely satisfactory (non-cutting blade, tricky grip, fragile sheath, etc.) one Major MacNary presented a completely different knife, which was accepted and named the "Trench Knife Mark I" or "Model 1918," that its designer had registered in Great Britain in October 1918. The blade was neither more nor less than that of the "Avenger of 1870." The grip, including knuckle-duster, was now in solid brass, and there were three successive models of sheath.

Since the American manufacturers were not yet able to produce this new knife, the contract was handed to the French SGCO firm, which explains the "lion" mark on the first models!

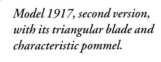

Model 1917, second version, with its triangular blade and characteristic pommel.

Designed by two renowned specialists

The famous manual of Major Fairbairn.

One of the many versions, with its very characteristic handle.

There is no detail of the hard reality of war that goes unnoticed by military professionals, for whom not only victory but their own lives are at stake. They must undergo constant training, know about all kinds of combat techniques and possess the best possible equipment. The two British Majors William Ewart Fairbairn and Eric Anthony Sykes both had long postings to Shanghai, where they were responsible for training the local police, who had to patrol the street and populous areas, in hand-to-hand fighting. The reputation of these two officers in this field was considerable. When they were recalled to Britain at the start of the Second World War and promoted to captain, they found themselves posted to the commando training center at Achnacarry in Scotland.

But the combat knives then available were considered totally unsatisfactory by Captain Fairbairn, and unsuited to the kinds of efficient techniques with which he had experimented in Shanghai in true combat situations. Having succeeded in convincing the general staff of the lack of an effective combat knife, in 1940 the two specialists set about designing a new model as fast as they could with the logistical support of the Wilkinson Sword Company. In 1941, a thousand of the first model of the Fairbairn & Sykes dagger were produced: a very slim, double-edged dagger blade, a two-quillon guard and rocket-shaped handle, in metal, with anti-slip ridges, for undeniable robustness and effectiveness!

In April 1941, a second version saw the light of day, followed by a third model at the start of 1943, with a few modifications rather than improvements. With more than a hundred thousand manufactured during the war, this dagger enjoyed unbelievable success with various British units and on a world scale was the most copied.

The Trench Knife US MK 3

A rigid sheath was also supplied: the US M.8.

Forever associated with the Normandy landings

T he most popular knife of the American army is undoubtedly the M3 model that reached France for the first time during the Normandy landings. Up until then the standard model had been the MK 1, but since this proved to be rather unsatisfactory, the military liaison officer in Indonesia made a request, in 1941, for a different type. That was how the MK 3 was born, in 1943, inspired by a shape of blade in use a century before.

The blade is long and straight, with a reverse-edge. The cylindrically-shaped handle is composed of slices of leather pressed together and then marked with regular grooves for better grip, particularly with wet hands. A flat, steel pommel sits atop this handle, while the end of the tang is riveted rather than screwed. The guard is formed from two flat, steel quillons, one of which turns down toward the point

The Trench Knife US MK 3, recognizable by its guard, of which one of the quillons is turned down toward the point.

The leather sheath is reinforced by two metal plates at the point.

of the blade.

The beautiful, leather sheath, identified by the reference "US M.6," is flat, sewn, and reinforced on both sides by metal claws. There are also two metal plates fixed either side of the point with four rivets. They serve to prevent the sheath being pierced in the event of a fall or landing, and wounding the soldier. Another sheath was also made, but in green plastic, the "US M.8."

Manufacture ceased in 1944, but since the 2,590,247 models produced had not all been distributed, the surplus was sold to various countries. That is how numerous French officers and legionnaires serving in Indochina and Algeria came to be wearing this knife at their belt, although in a French-made leather sheath.

US MK 3

A combat knife for special missions

The current firm, SOG knives, proposes two models on which all details are scrupulously respected.

T he Vietnam War was fought in the most unusual conditions, whether they be technical, strategic or climatic. On the ground, apart from the regular armies, there were various "phantom" units, whose task involved the planning and undertaking of secret missions in the whole of Southeast Asia. One of these was the Military Assistance Command Vietnam—Studies and Observations Group, known by its initials SOG. The CIA aided and advised this new organization in its sabotage and psychological warfare missions and other special operations in both North and South Vietnam, as well as in Laos, Cambodia and the South of China. The SOG, comprised of men drawn from the Special Forces of the United States Army, developed specific equipment and weaponry, including a combat knife in different variants intended exclusively for its members.

Considered by specialists as one of the finest examples of the genre, the basic version consists of an imposing blade with a reverse-edge and either brushed or black phosphate to avoid any reflection that might attract the attention of the enemy. A sturdy brass guard with two quillons provides an effective protection; the handle was made of slices of leather, with finger outlines for a better grip; a metal pommel fixed by a screw enabled complete disassembly. The black leather sheath was fitted with a pocket containing sharpening materials, that is to say a stone or small steel.

When the American Army returned home, this knife did not fail to attract attention, and so it happened that two specialized brands, Al Mar and SOG knives, came to reproduce it admirably to the great pleasure of collectors everywhere.

Al Mar has reproduced the original model perfectly.

Traditional model in sheath.

For survival after the crash…

U. S. Navy pilots have always fought everywhere. After the Second World War came Korea, where weather conditions were far from comfortable, but this was nothing compared to what awaited them in Vietnam. There they found hostile vegetation, heat, torrential rain and constant humidity. Flying over immense stretches of territory, they frequently risked a crash landing or else a descent by parachute from a burning aircraft.

So as to be able to survive in such inhospitable environments, pilots were meticulously equipped by the Navy. A knife was an essential part of this equipment. But the models left over from the Second World War were found wanting, and so Marble's Arms Corp. was awarded the task of designing this new knife, which it started to produce in 1957. With a complete length of 27.9 cm,

the blade was of a Bowie shape with a reverse-edge. Saw-teeth on the back enabled branches and the like to be cut easier. The guard has two quillons, with the handle made of slices of leather fixed by a steel pommel in the shape of a large screw, often covered in fluorescent paint. The sheath was in leather, with a cord enabling it to be carried in various ways, and a small pocket containing a sharpening stone.

Since Marble's could not meet the huge volume of orders, Utica, Camillus, Milpar and Kiffe were then asked to produce large quantities, with slightly shorter blades of 25 cm.

This knife, inseparable companion for all missions, is wreathed in a thousand and one legends, having enabled numerous pilots to survive in places where, without it, survival would have been impossible.

Air Force pilot survival knife.

An ultramodern vision of the combat knife

The "willow-leaf" shape of the blade is most characteristic. So as to meet specific requirements it was given an angle, with phosphate and sawtooth versions.

During the long Vietnam War, there was a considerable demand for equipment of all kinds, and there were many companies who, either by patriotic fervor or commercial interest, produced accessories that the army did not supply. Gerber, whose hunting and outdoor knives were greatly appreciated, set out to design a combat model, calling on the services of Bud Holzman, a retired captain.

Holzman developed a dagger prototype which was greatly modified after tests on the ground. The first models were manufactured in 1967. Strongly influenced by the famous duo of Fairbairn & Sykes, this dagger has a flatter blade though, with a willow-leaf shape, a gray metal handle and a solid guard with two quillons. The sheath is in leather.

The blade became more rounded later on, and was produced in black, with saw-teeth cut into the blade halfway up on both sides. With these new "survival" features the knife was renamed the Mark II Survival Knife in 1979.

More than a hundred thousand were made and immediately sold. The Special Forces could not ignore the effectiveness of such a weapon and different variants were made according to specific requests from various units: the handle was produced in different colors (yellow, orange, etc.) and in other, lighter materials. In addition, to meet hand-to-hand combat requirements, certain blades were produced with the blade extending from the guard at an angle so that the point would be turned away off-center. Along with the Fairbairn & Sykes dagger, the Gerber Mark II is certainly the most copied model in the world, which attests to its renown.

Numerous models were made. The black leather sheath was slowly replaced by a tawny-colored one. As for the handle, it also had variants in black, yellow or orange.

Present on all fronts!

Units of the Special Forces were frequently equipped with the n°1.

When the Second World War broke out, Bo Randall, who would later become one of the most famous knifemakers on the planet, had not been forging knives for long, and only hunting, fishing and outdoor models. Seizing the opportunity that was offered him, he designed a completely original combat knife: a long 8-inch blade, slim with a reverse-edge, a brass guard with double quillon and a handle of pressed leather slices held in place by an aluminum pommel screwed to the tang. The leather sheath had a small pocket containing a sharpening stone.

Every model in the catalogue had a name and number; this one was called the "All Purpose Fighting Knife" and was given the number "1."

With the assistance of an experienced bladesmith and two workers, more than three thousand were produced from 1942 in the little Florida workshop. But in view of the backlog of outstanding orders, he was obliged to sub-contract to a small company in Springfield, Massachusetts, which supplied exactly 1,058 of this model to Europe. Among the privileged few who received one of these famous models were numerous personalities, including a certain Air Force captain who certainly never suspected at the time what dizzy heights

he would one day attain— Ronald Reagan!

When the United States actively joined the Vietnam War in 1965, there were once more huge orders of the n°1 model; again some of the production had to be sub-contracted, despite a better organization of the workshop and increased number of employees. This time it was to Solingen, in Germany, that they turned.

Bo Randall was already a legend; the n°1 swiftly followed him!

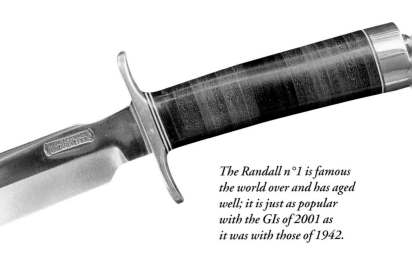

The Randall n°1 is famous the world over and has aged well; it is just as popular with the GIs of 2001 as it was with those of 1942.

The last chance knife…

The boot knife is short, but robust and most effective.

The first modern combat knife was the bayonet, as soon as its means of fixation evolved from a rod slipped into a socket, into an actual handle that enabled a hitherto impossible grip. Combat daggers were soon produced in a wide variety of styles, with each country favoring a particular detail over another, a particular shape or material…

In general, the handle was designed to be grabbed hold of quickly and effectively, even when raining, with a double-quillon guard fitted to prevent the fingers from slipping onto the blade. The blade, of a reasonable length, was either double-edged for the dagger models, or else reverse-edged for the knife models. Such knives were carried in sheaths made from leather, canvas or any other rigid material, and attached to the belt or webbing, which meant that wherever it was carried it was always visible.

The boot knife, as it name suggests, is discreetly carried in the boot, which may appear strange but actually makes perfect sense. In certain circumstances where the slightest movement counts, the boot is often much easier to reach than the belt. Also, when all hope seems lost, a hidden blade can get you out of a sticky situation, which is why in the U.S. this type of knife is called the "last chance" knife. The boot knife is thus undoubtedly a modern combat knife and part of the equipment of all elite units, but the idea is not new, the principle having appeared in Scotland in 1745 with the skean dhu.

Clipped to the inside of the boot…

An integral part of the legend of the Old West

As surprising as it may seem, at the end of the 18th century and beginning of the 19th, there was not a single knifemaker in all America, despite the large numbers of people swarming all over it…all over that is except for the West, which was still too wild to venture into. The few metalsmiths concentrated essentially on plowing implements, horseshoes and odd repairs, but rarely the manufacture of blades. It was thus logical for the colonizers to look to their countries of origin for all cutlery requirements. The principal supplier was England. Apart from folding knives and various all-purpose straight models pro-

Bison had to be cut up to feed the railway construction workers.

duced in the purest Sheffield style, it soon became necessary to create specific shapes to meet the requirements encountered in this vast New World. One of these requirements was skinning animals to make clothes, and so it was that the I. Wilson firm designed one of the first "skinner" type knives in 1750.

In 1818, Henry Harrington established the first cutlery factory on the continent, followed, in 1834, by John Russell, whose clientele was now much larger than that of his predecessor. Descended from an old family of English pioneers, John Russell chose the banks of the Green River, near Greenfield, Massachusetts, to set up his first factory, to the great astonishment of his family and friends. In fact, John did not have the slightest experience in this domain, his first activity having been as a silversmith, followed by cotton in Georgia, where he amassed a considerable fortune. In 1832, he made a trip back down memory lane to his birthplace and decided to set up home there and take early retirement. The place was so devoid of activity, though, that his only escape from depression was to throw himself into a new professional occupation! But why knifemaking? There was no tradition of it in the country and he himself had no knowledge of the craft. Unfortunately history cannot enlighten us. Perhaps he just said to himself: "Why not?"

Successive failures, like the destruction of the factory on two occasions by fire and once by the flooding of the Green River, and the great difficulty in finding

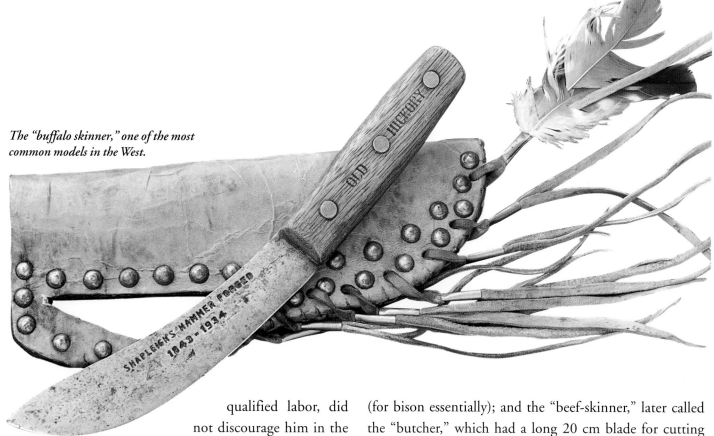

The "buffalo skinner," one of the most common models in the West.

qualified labor, did not discourage him in the slightest. He also produced wooden tools that he sold through his brother Francis, who had the idea of opening a shop in New York. So when the first series of long knives was launched, there was already an excellent sales outlet based there in the East, from which it spread out through the interior of the continent.

This first series comprised five models, all of which are still sold today! Carefully planned manufacturing methods ensured a very large production, with the nearby river providing hydraulic energy for the power hammers. The materials were also of the highest quality, originating from Sheffield. Of an extremely simple flat-sole design with two riveted wooden plaques for the handle, they were also intended for particular use: skinning and cutting-up animals. These included the "buffalo-skinner," with its characteristic wide point that turns up; the "Dadley Universal," which was an early "utility" knife; a boning knife; a "semi-skinner," which was easier for cutting up and skinning medium game than its big brother

(for bison essentially); and the "beef-skinner," later called the "butcher," which had a long 20 cm blade for cutting up meat. Many other models were produced, for trappers, mountain men and anglers. There was a hardly a single one of those great adventurers of the heyday of the Old West who had never used one of the famous Green River blades!

Two other short-bladed Green River models.

A "beef-skinner" with its long blade.

| # The knife of the Native Americans

Before and after the arrival of the white man

The Native American on horseback, hunting bison with a bow and arrow is an image rendered by numerous artists, although the reality was somewhat different.

Since the movement of human beings was characteristic of both the pre and proto-historic periods, it was natural that the American continent also experienced population movement. Tribes were formed and eventually settled, opting for a particular site or way of life. From the frozen north of Canada right down to Mexico, through swamp, mountain, plain, desert, lake or river, these tribes multiplied: Seminole, Creek, Yuma, Cheyenne, Apache, Cherokee, Comanche, Navajo, Hopi, Sioux are the most well known of the ones that survived. But there were many others, some of whom have now disappeared forever: Sauk, Mandan, Blackfoot, Kansas, Yoway, Mohican, Huron, Pequot, Mohawk, Narragansett, Pakanoket, Shawnee, Iroquois, Crowh, Algonquin, to name but a few.

Although pottery, basketry and weaving were soon mastered, metallurgy was always ignored by these Native Americans, as surprising as it may seem. They were fond of producing superb clothes decorated with beads, of painting and sculpting some of their objects, but they only worked silver for decorative purposes and never touched iron. Spear and arrowheads were cut from flint, obsidian or bone. For a club, they lashed a stone to a shaft of wood, or else wielded particularly fearsome pieces of antler or bone. It is understandable that the shields with which they protected themselves during tribal conflicts were made of bison hide since that provided sufficient protection against such weapons, although they were of little use against steel arrowheads.

There is no rational theory to explain why metallurgy, which appeared 3,000 B.C. on all the other continents, did not reach North America, unless it was simply not part of the culture or tradition of its native inhabitants.

The first metal blades appeared only in the 16th century, when contacts started to evolve between Europeans and the Native Americans. The principle of barter soon appeared, with English, Dutch, French and Spanish colonizers supplying various objects, including knives, in exchange for hides. These knives slowly replaced those made from flint, obsidian and bone, since the advantages of this new material were soon realized.

*Long blades
served not only for
cutting up bison,
but also for combat…*

*The Native Americans
held a particular affection
for certain materials for
making their knife handles,
including bone.*

It was only in 1830 that the Native Americans, due to their contact with the European colonizers, started to learn the craft of the smithy, first attempting to modify certain blades before making them from scratch, not from raw minerals, but from scraps of steel that they found, mostly from files and grinders. These knives generally lacked a guard, and the handles were made from natural materials like wood, bone or horn, but always worked in the purest Native American style. There were even example of a bear's jaw being used as a handle, no doubt to demonstrate the strength and courage of its owner.

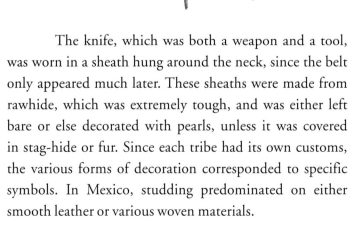

*Native
Americans are
Old Masters
in the art
of beading.*

The knife, which was both a weapon and a tool, was worn in a sheath hung around the neck, since the belt only appeared much later. These sheaths were made from rawhide, which was extremely tough, and was either left bare or else decorated with pearls, unless it was covered in stag-hide or fur. Since each tribe had its own customs, the various forms of decoration corresponded to specific symbols. In Mexico, studding predominated on either smooth leather or various woven materials.

A man and a knife, both most distinguished

Jim Bowie.

Jim Bowie, born in Logan County, Kentucky, in 1796, was a sturdy fellow, 6 feet tall and weighing 180 pounds, whose reputation as a womanizer was equaled only by his reputation as an inveterate fighter. The story of his heroic death at Fort Alamo on the 6th of March 1836 alongside Davy Crockett, is one of the great stories of bravery in American legend. His courage and skill with a knife made him one of the top experts in such weapons; from there it was but a short step to designing new forms of blade…

In the course of the year 1830 he developed a completely original design, the wooden model of which he gave to James Black, a renowned bladesmith of Washington, Arkansas, requesting that the knife be produced within nineteen days. Black scrupulously respected all of the details, but holding his client in high esteem and considering that the proposed design had certain flaws, he made a second version according to his own design, even forging the blade from a meteorite that he had been saving for such an exceptional occasion! When Jim came to collect his knife he was presented with the two models and asked to choose which one he wanted, for no additional cost. He chose the second one… It was this very same knife that he was carrying at the Alamo, and which disappeared with him in the ensuing battle.

A "Bowie" is a straight knife, with a particularly long and powerful blade that also has a most characteristic shape, particularly the part where the reverse-edge curves up. "Bowie" became synonymous with large-blade knives and this genre is particularly sought after in the United States even today, but opinions differ considerably concerning the characteristics of the original model. At the time it was common to carry a large straight-knife at one's belt, and Jim Bowie was certainly no exception, never missing an opportunity to "clash swords." He is credited with a fair number of fights and even duels, the most famous of which took place on the 19th of September 1827 at Avoyelles-Rapides Parishes, Louisiana (this is an historical fact).

But a number of writings belonging to Jim's brother Rezin were conserved in a museum. In one of them he mentions that: "The first Bowie knife was made by myself in Avoyelles Parish; it was intended only for hunting and I carried it for several years; the blade was 23 centimeters long and 4 wide, with a single cutting edge and not curved…"

Rezin then added several modifications and improvements before getting a number of knives made by a local smith. Apparently it was one of these knives that Jim used for his most famous duel, as well as another one against a certain Sturdivant, who was only wounded and

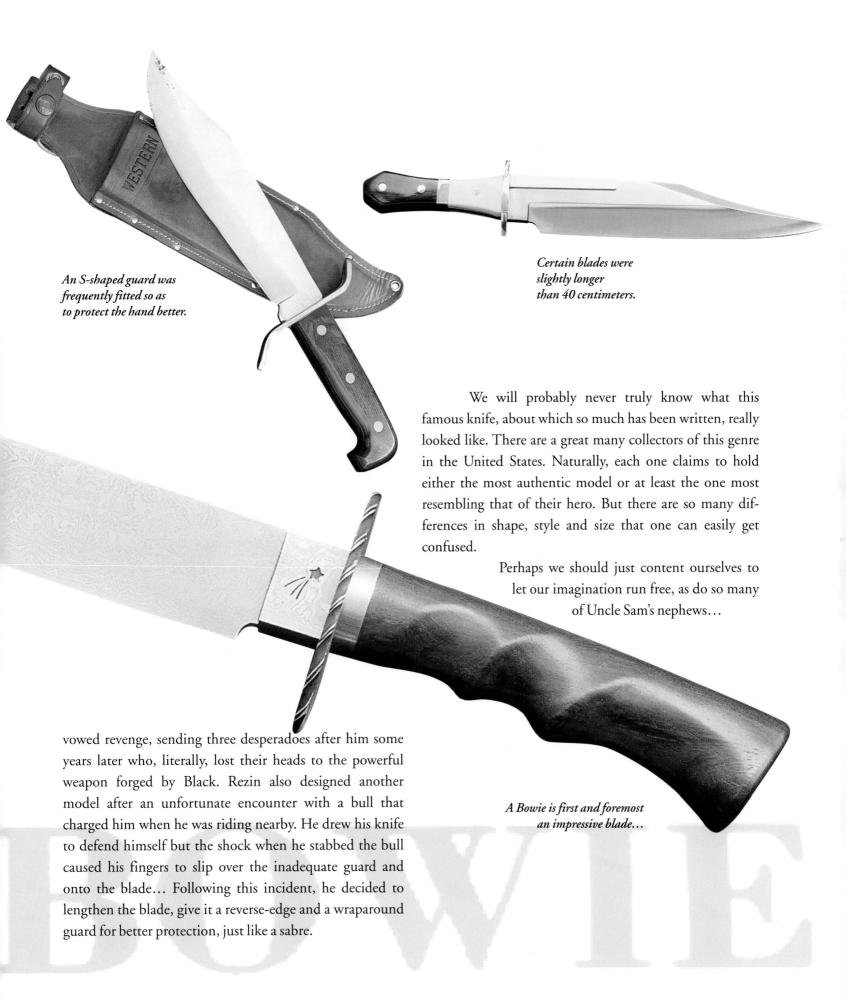

An S-shaped guard was frequently fitted so as to protect the hand better.

Certain blades were slightly longer than 40 centimeters.

We will probably never truly know what this famous knife, about which so much has been written, really looked like. There are a great many collectors of this genre in the United States. Naturally, each one claims to hold either the most authentic model or at least the one most resembling that of their hero. But there are so many differences in shape, style and size that one can easily get confused.

Perhaps we should just content ourselves to let our imagination run free, as do so many of Uncle Sam's nephews…

A Bowie is first and foremost an impressive blade…

vowed revenge, sending three desperadoes after him some years later who, literally, lost their heads to the powerful weapon forged by Black. Rezin also designed another model after an unfortunate encounter with a bull that charged him when he was riding nearby. He drew his knife to defend himself but the shock when he stabbed the bull caused his fingers to slip over the inadequate guard and onto the blade… Following this incident, he decided to lengthen the blade, give it a reverse-edge and a wraparound guard for better protection, just like a sabre.

Refined elegance...

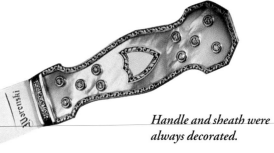

Handle and sheath were always decorated.

From 1850, a number of major cutlery factories were established, mainly in Massachusetts and Connecticut, and dozens of little workshops sprang up all over the country. Soon every major town boasted local production of both knives and surgical instruments. Every knifemaker, whatever the volume of production, developed a type of knife according to demand, that is to say for domestic use or one of the numerous outdoor activities, but the style varied little from one manufacturer to another.

Until the 1840's, San Francisco was an obscure little village of just a few hundred inhabitants, but its tranquility and anonymity ceased with the influx of prospectors, the gold rush having turned the place into a major strategic point. Houses sprouted up everywhere. Vice was not long to follow...

Returning home at night was no risk-free venture, since every dark street corner held a potential ambush, whether the aggressor be simply a drunk after a few coins, a gambler who had just lost everything, an unlucky gold-digger or a professional thief.

Bankers, preachers, merchants and farmers rarely carried a gun. But they often had a knife at their belt for defense against these frequent attacks. The most elegant of these individuals would never have dreamed of equipping themselves with the same kind of blade as carried by outdoor fellows. No, they required luxury, personalized models, with ivory handles decorated with silver inlay. The sheath itself was often made from this noble metal. The "Old San Francisco" style was born, created by various cutler-silversmiths whose legacy of finely crafted knives attests to their skill.

An "Old San Francisco" knife is elegance above all.

The knife of the professional gambler

I n this America where opportunities were vast, towns grew at a vertiginous rate as soon as populations reached critical mass. Every kind of commerce was doing a roaring trade and all kinds of distraction and entertainment were available for the cowboys, who had been breathing the dust kicked up by their herds of cattle for months on end, often staying up to eighteen hours in the saddle a day. After a good bath, a trip to the barber and a great slap-up meal to wipe away the monotony of the daily diet of beans, they only had to slope through the swing doors of saloon bars to find loose women and high-stakes galore! No man willingly accepts to lose his money, particularly when somewhat inebriated or when the dandy opposite has displayed an excess of arrogance! It is just a small step to accusations of cheating, regularly expressed at all gaming tables during those long, hot nights.

Whether a cheat or not, professional gamblers were often targets. Always on their guard, ritually placing their backs to the wall so as to face any attack, they carried a twin-barrel Derringer in the pocket of their waistcoat with a "push dagger" slipped in their belt.

Discreet, and easily accessible, this push dagger had a short, pointed double-edged blade with a T-shaped handle providing good grip. The sheath was generally metallic. Knives of this type appeared for the first time in San Francisco, with local cutlers embellishing them with wonderful silverwork that did not detract, however, from their terrible effectiveness.

Metal sheath with belt clip for rapid unsheathing…

Certain models were particularly luxurious.

111

For the bartering with the Indians

The vast American territories contained diverse resources that were exploited as soon as they were discovered. So it was that in 1807 a fur merchant named Manuel Lisa foresaw what could become a pelt empire. He established the first trading post on the Yellowstone to handle all of the skins in the region, but in doing so he blazed a trail that would stretch beyond the Rocky Mountains. There was no lack of furry animals on the continent, primarily beavers, but also gray, brown and black bears, as well as the enormous grizzlies, raccoons, lynxes, wildcats, silver and red foxes, wolves, coyotes, weasels, badgers, martens, otters, minks, ermines, polecats, wolverines, muskrats, sables, marmots, and squirrels, as well as mountain goats, mouflon sheep, moose, wapitis, and of course bison… Such a plethora of wildlife and potential pelts could not escape the attention of the governments of the various colonizing powers, England in particular. Two English trading companies were established in Oregon, the North-West Company and the Hudson Bay Company, whose goal was to collect as many pelts as possible

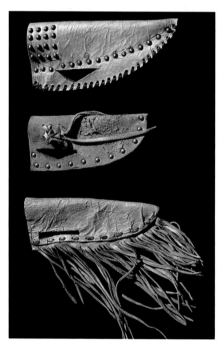

Styles of sheath vary according to tribe, from fringes to studding and beading…

and transport them back to England by sea. The number of pelts handled by these companies in the years up to 1840 was impressive. The famous "skin book," in which all transactions were noted, is most edifying on this point.

More than two hundred forts were built to safeguard transactions, which gives an idea of the extent of the operation, that played an important role in the development of the continent. This trade gave birth to a new type of individual, the "mountain man," a fearsome trapper who knew his territory like the back of his hand, living on his own in the wild for months on end, after which time he would haul his pelts to the nearest fort either to sell them or exchange them for supplies, which might run from whisky to a rifle and powder, a canoe, or a knife!

The Native Americans were also tempted to trade their pelts, which is how they were able to procure either knives or simply blades that they mounted on handles of their own manufacture. They were also greatly interested in tools, which they used for working the land, and started to make

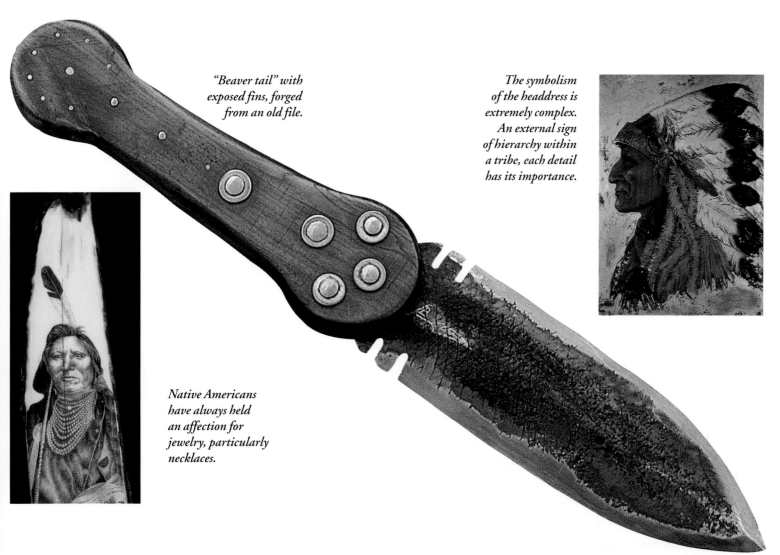

"Beaver tail" with exposed fins, forged from an old file.

The symbolism of the headdress is extremely complex. An external sign of hierarchy within a tribe, each detail has its importance.

Native Americans have always held an affection for jewelry, particularly necklaces.

modifications to them after learning some of the secrets of the forge. This is how knives with large blades appeared, as well as metal spearheads. Hatchets intended for chopping wood were turned into fearsome tomahawks and pipes of peace.

The type of knife most representative of this period of trade with the Hudson Bay Company is undoubtedly the "beaver-tail" knife.

At this time, the vast majority of knives in the territories came from Sheffield, and certainly those traded by the company, since it was English. The shapes and sizes that suited the pioneers' requirements the best were frequently developed and had nothing in common with the usual production. Having received an order for rustic blades to trade with the Native Americans, the English bladesmiths opted for a "spearhead" model, sharpened on both sides. One series was flat-sole, while another was mounted on a tang with two transversal fins. Nothing

was simpler than fitting a handle to the flat-sole and the tang to a shaft to make a spear, the fins enabling a sturdy ligature. But these two fins did not in any way prevent the blade from being used as a knife. When the company eventually closed, the Native Americans forged this kind of blade themselves from old files. But in both Canada and America such models were later produced by various manufacturers, which explains why so many of them were traded to tribes who had great difficulty in mastering the special technique required to produce double-edged blades. Numerous engravings from the period show a brave or a chief carrying a beaver tail in a sheath slung around his neck, stuck in his belt, on the end of a spear-shaft or even on a "gunstock," one of those sinister clubs that they wielded so artfully.

The beaver tail is certainly a fine representative object of this legendary time in American history!

Its origin is still a mystery…

In the chapter on the 1900's in his monumental work *Cutlery from its Origins to the Present Day,* Camille Page writes: "Estaing knives: knives with this name were designed in 1780 by Admiral Estaing for use on board his ship; they can be used for dining, for cutting or for defense." There is some doubt though as to the true origins of this highly original knife that is no more no less than a straight folding knife, a first of its kind since up until then knives had been either straight or folding, but certainly never both at the same time! But let us attempt to penetrate the veil of mystery by exploring the legend of this unusual character.

Born in the castle of Ravel (Puy-de-Dôme) in 1729, Count Charles Henri d'Estaing joined the military establishment at a very young age. Musketeer to the king in 1738, aide-de-camp of the Maréchal de Saxe in 1742, he was promoted to Captain in the Rouergue regiment in 1745 at just fifteen years old… Wounded for the first time during the War of Flanders, he was promoted to major in 1747 and two years later became ambassador's secretary to the English Court. Soon he was in America, followed by the West Indies and Pondichery. He participated in the taking of Madras (during which he was again wounded) and then went to Réunion. Appointed governor of the Leeward Islands, then vice admiral of the seas of Asia and Africa, he played a heroic part in the American War of Independence, took Grenada in 1779 and was wounded once more in Savannah. Appointed governor of Touraine, he became commander of the French National Guard in that terrible year of 1789 (The French Revolution), before finally being promoted admiral of France in 1794. However, he was arrested on the 28th of April of the same year during the Great Terror and guillotined, despite his republican and avant-garde convictions.

Estaing sailed all over the world and was clearly a man whose sixty-five years of life were amply-filled. He was curious about everything. How could one not be in this century of Enlightenment that saw such illustrious names as Diderot, Rousseau, Voltaire, Montesquieu, Bach, George

With the handle folded, part of the blade is still useable.

Some added a corkscrew.

Every manufacturer developed its own locking and release mechanism for the blade.

Modern version of the famous dagger.

sitting down at a table to consume it, after having folded the blade back down to a manageable size. It makes for easier carrying, enabling one to have an effective weapon for self-defense since the admiral was rarely far from the front-line.

Washington and Benjamin Franklin? A freemason, interested in both symbolism and the hidden side of things, it was clear that not just any knife would do for this man! The original model has never been found, and we have no detailed description of it. However, we can get quite a precise idea from the two models from this era exhibited in the Cutlery Museum of Thiers: one is composed of a long blade with an ivory handle that swivels on an axis to partially fold over this blade. The handle of the second model does not pivot; instead the blade slides partially into the handle, enabling it to be used in the position required. Why such a particularity? Well, certainly for the simple pleasure and originality of it, but also for convenience: this knife enables one to carve a superb leg of lamb before

But was such a mechanism the fruit of his own imagination? Or was it inspired by "secret" knives? Or from "butterfly" models seen in the West Indies during one of his voyages? Or else from knives seen in London or America? Unfortunately, Admiral Estaing took this secret with him to his grave.

The ingenuity of such a system certainly did not escape the notice of the cutlers of Thiers, which was not far from the admiral's estate. They modernized this knife to make it suitable for hunting, and today this is a particularly popular model.

Forged for African adventures…

A corkscrew was placed in the spring of the switchblade mechanism.

What a fascinating character Ernest Hemingway was… Journalist, war correspondent, writer and Nobel Prize winner, he was born in Illinois in 1899 and burned the candle of his sixty-two years at both ends…. He roamed the world, sailed the seven seas and was sensitive to everything and everyone he encountered. A big-game hunter, he made many trips to Africa, particularly Kenya and Tanzania, which inspired him to write *The Snows of Kilimanjaro.* Each of his safaris was an adventure in itself, at a time when there were many lands still untouched by "civilization." In the bush, facing every kind of danger, it was essential to have a powerful and reliable gun, as well as an excellent knife. Legend recounts that this great hunter always chose the best when he armed himself. But although we know everything about his guns, from brand to caliber, it is only due to the stroke of fortune that placed a certain boutique in his path, that we know anything at all about his knives.

The Kindals have been knifemakers for generations in Sweden, but one of them decided to move to Paris, to the very swanky Avenue de l'Opéra, number 33. On the font of the shop was a sign spelling out in white lettering: "Grinding." In the 1950s, Hemingway was living in the Paris Ritz, which is not far from this boutique, and so passed in front of it several times a day. One fine morning he entered and handed Mr. Kindal a knife to be sharpened. Impressed by the quality of the object's finish, our Swedish cutler was inspired to make an identical copy of it.

Hemingway gave him his full assent, even agreeing to let Kindal name the knife after him! Ever since then this famous "Hemingway" model has been specially made by the Kindal firm. The model is noticeable for its ivory-capped pommel on the stag-antler handle. There is one main blade with switchblade mechanism, a shorter blade, a saw and of course a corkscrew.

The "Hemingway" in all its glory!

Faithful companion of the valiant Himalayan Gurkhas

The kukri is fearsomely effective.

Nepal. This tiny state to the north of India, with just twenty million inhabitants, evokes Katmandu, the Himalayas and of course Mount Everest... A close neighbor of Tibet, this reputedly peaceful country has a fearsome military caste, whose members are known as Gurkhas.

During the Anglo-Nepalese War of 1814-1816, the British soldiers who brushed with them were deeply impressed by their bravery and fighting spirit. Although beaten—due to the superior numbers of British troops and the experience they had acquired in India—they made peace with their adversaries, who saw a unique chance to swell their ranks with these high-quality soldiers and recruited them immediately.

Since then more than 250,000 Gurkhas have served under the Union Jack on all fronts.

Their first noteworthy engagement in the service of Her Majesty was during the Indian Mutiny of 1857. In the Great War, they were present from Mesopotamia to the Marne. Indeed it was the Gurkhas who broke the Turkish lines at Gallipoli! During the Second World War they helped kick Rommel out of North Africa and took part in the horrific jungle fighting against the Japanese from Burma to Malaya. In the Falklands, two Argentinean companies preferred to surrender to the Scot's Guards rather than face an onslaught from these stocky warriors who are rarely taller than 5'3".

Their famous fighting dagger is the kukri. Legend tells that it cannot be sheathed until it has been whetted with the blood of an enemy in combat. Ever faithful to the crown, the Gurkhas are just as loyal to their famous kukri, which they hold in their left hand with the point raised when presenting arms. A dagger whose shape and forging techniques are lost in the heights of the Himalayas…

The kukri did not go unnoticed by the famous Randall workshop.

Symbol of this warrior sect

A kirpan is always a luxurious object.

Jot S. Khalsa is highly reputed in the production of Sikh daggers.

At the end of the 15th century there were many in the North-West of the Indian subcontinent who wondered whether a formalized and ritualistic religion, like the Hinduism or Islam that they practiced, could truly bring them closer to God. Sikhism, which was starting to gain ground, seemed to offer another way.

The guru Nanak, who lived from 1469 to 1539, founded the Sikh religious movement in the Punjab. Although it was initially a community of devotees united by a search for God, a powerful military organization was soon established to keep order as their followers continued to grow. Sikhism thus became assimilated very early on with a sort of military theocracy. Development of physical fitness was an important part of an initiate's training, with competitions organized among disciples! These activities were intended essentially for physical training and not for combat, but they certainly constituted a military training, which proved to be particularly effective when subjected to violent attacks from Muslims.

Of course the war with Islam did not concern only the Sikhs, but the whole of the Punjab. The Sikhs, however, were the dominant military force. It is clear that the Sikh religion had the goal of leading man away from the self-importance, ignorance and selfishness in which he was foundering, to an awareness of the Great Divinity and consequently the value of his own life, for which they considered the appropriate path to be martial rather than contemplative.

Among the five distinctive signs identifying a Sikh is a dagger called a "kirpan," which is worn either at the belt or else fixed to the cuff. Sikhs have never hesitated to use it either. Indeed they have often been entrusted with some of the most important roles in the Indian defense forces due to their respected warrior tradition.

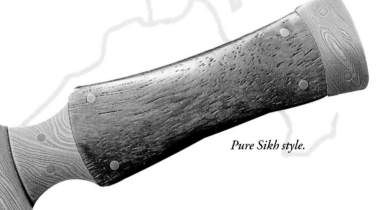

Pure Sikh style.

A blade with strange powers

Awaveform blade evoking the sacred serpent Naga; such is the kriss, this long dagger that appeared first of all in Malaysia, then from the 15th century in Java. Such a type of blade is unique, and in these countries rich in beliefs and symbols, its originality is not just limited to its shape. The kriss leads us into a world full of mystery…

More than just a dagger, the kriss is a ritual object, not to be forged by just anyone! No, only an empu can do that, a bladesmith instructed in secrets revealed to him during a long initiatory period; a man considered even to possess magical powers. The forge is constructed according to ancestral principles and cannot be built just anywhere: the mountain summit permits a better communication with the spirits. The very blade itself is imbued with a soul, and one needs more than technique to draw it in… The right metals must be used, producing a particular marbling effect called a *pamor.*

The *empu* cannot start his work at just any moment either. The special day is scrupulously chosen according to a multitude of complex considerations. The first phase of the work may only take place after a process of purification, with each step preceded by offerings. The tiniest detail—the shape of the flame or the direction of the wind that particular day—are of utmost importance. Once the blade has been finished, its upper part will undergo chiseling, with the choice of motifs again subject to various esoteric subtleties, with a respect for harmony reigning over the whole undertaking. A wooden handle, or ukiran, will be fixed, at the base of which collars will be placed after they have been decorated by a silversmith. Finally a sheath, or *wrangha,* will be fashioned in wood. Intended to guarantee the link between heaven and the man who wears it, the kriss not only keeps demons at bay, the powers given to it are even more powerful…

The kriss is much more than just a blade.

Specially designed for space

When astronauts embark onboard their vessel to accomplish another space mission, all of their equipment is generally at the cutting-edge of technology. But how could one really imagine that NASA technicians would place such importance from the very start in an item of personal equipment that was not of an electronic nature; a simple knife! Man has always headed off to conquer other territories, first of all by necessity, then by a desire for discovery, freedom and challenge. The first migrations were actually a question of survival. It was necessary to flee a region or climate that had become hostile; by the same token it was essential to follow the migrations of animals in order to feed oneself. But development of settled civilizations has never shaken man's passion for discovering new territories, across land and sea, from the highest mountains to the deepest oceans. Then came the skies, the planets, the Universe and infinity…

Mankind's genes contain this thirst for conquest and discovery, but none of these adventures were ever launched without the best material suitable for the journey to be undertaken. From Cro-Magnon man to Neil Armstrong, man's faithful travelling companion has been a knife. Carried everywhere this little object is undoubtedly useful in a variety of situations, on land or at sea, but one might well wonder what usefulness a knife might have in the high-tech environment of space-exploration and travel.

In fact there are a number of little jobs on board a space vessel that can be admirably undertaken with a multi-blade knife, including making emergency repairs that will ensure the success of the mission, as numerous official accounts have proven.

The "Swiss Army Master Craftsman" was used by Payton on board the space shuttle Discovery to undertake work on navigational equipment, leading Victorinox to produce an "Astronaut" model intended exclusively for members of NASA, of which the nearest equivalent commercially available is the "Ranger," reference 1.3763. This immediately led to the other Swiss firm, Wenger, developing a specific model,

The "Astro" by Randall; a benchmark...

and these two brands became official NASA suppliers. But although the mission consists essentially of going into space, the return to earth should certainly not be forgotten. The re-entry trajectory can undergo last-minute alterations that could result in the vessel landing not at Cape Canaveral, but perhaps in the middle of the African bush or Amazon rain forest.

In such a case, a "survival" type knife is essential. Moreover, crew members regularly undergo training in these inhospitable environments, enabling them to familiarize themselves with the equipment made at their disposal. Different types of knife have thus been tested under true conditions, particularly in the jungle of Panama. The first model was developed by Bo Randall after being con-

tacted by Major Gordon Cooper, who was aware of the fine models produced by the Randall workshop for numerous élite units for various conflicts.

The "Astro" was based on the n° 15 or "Airman" model, and was officially adopted in October 1960. This knife accompanied Gordon Cooper, Alan Shepherd and Virgil Grissom in the course of the first American manned space missions. There was also a machete model produced by the Case company, which was taken into space for the first time in 1965, on board the *Molly Brown*.

Who will be the manufacturer of the knife that makes it to Mars?

For the ritual ceremonies

The throwing knife; a typically African genre.

Africa. Spellbinding, fascinating, mysterious… The Europeans were not able to resist its attraction, settling there for a century, starting in 1850. But this vast continent was home to a multitude of different peoples, whose ancestral traditions varied as much as the landscape.

Various beliefs and ceremonies require different clothes, but whatever the ethnic group, the dagger is always present, whether to accomplish a ritual gesture or to display one's strength or pride. Each of these daggers differs from its neighbor by its name, shape, materials and use.

In Morocco, the koumya holds sway, with its decorated wooden handle carried in a sliver-copper sheath that is curved at the end, whereas in the Atlas mountains the genoui with its straight blade is preferred. In Kabylia, the Berbers have long been faithful to the fissa, with its long, straight and slim blade. It has a wooden handle with a pommel that is sometimes carved to represent the head of a dog. The sheath is in decorated wood, with silverwork. In the Sahara the Touareg never go anywhere without their long sword, the takouba, and a dagger, the telek, with its characteristic cruciform hilt. Their manufacture is undoubtedly influenced by nearby Toledo.

In central Africa, models are extremely rudimentary, the characteristics

they share with those of North Africa being the mediocrity of the quality of iron or steel used for the blades, whose cutting edge blunts very rapidly.

In the Sudan we find a dagger that is attached to the forearm, the haussa. Throwing knives are particularly common in the Congo, with a shape that recalls the sickle, the hatchet and other tools used for working the land…

Many African knives are used for sacrifices, which explains why their blades are often long and curved. Every detail of their ornamentation corresponds to a symbol whose significance is handed down from generation to generation.

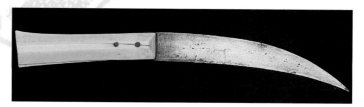

Sacrificial knife with a long curved blade and ivory handle.

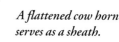

A flattened cow horn serves as a sheath.

A style and design all of its own

It is not uncommon to find certain models embellished with silver.

The German hunter is traditionally represented wearing a green hat and loden jacket, as well as leather pants laced at the calf. A closer look reveals a little pocket on the right-hand side, above the knee, from which emerges a pommel signaling the presence of a knife, which might seem rather strange. The current traditional dress of the Tyrol has not changed that much since the 16th century, with wide braces cut from the same leather as the heavy pants they hold up so effectively. Since a gut swollen by too much beer cannot reasonably be expected to accommodate a belt, how else can one carry a straight knife if not in a pocket specially conceived for the purpose?

This straight, typically Germanic knife is the nicker. Traces of it being carried in this way can be found as far back as the 16th century. Ever since then it has served well for any job. Light, fine and very pointed, it is mounted on a collar, forged from a single piece and fitted with a handle in stag's antler. The sheath is in leather, with metal decorations, and it only contains the blade so as not to damage the leather of the pants.

But why a fine and very pointed blade for a knife intended for every purpose? On one hand, the robustness does not depend on the thickness of the blade but rather on the quality of the steel used and the care taken during its forging, tempering and assembly. On the other hand, this knife was very soon used for hunting in a region that hunts essentially stags, roe deer and chamois. But when an animal is not killed on the spot, it must be put out of its misery as quickly and effectively as possible. Local practice consists of severing the spinal column at the nape of the neck, for which a very fine knife is essential.

Nacken is the German for "nape of the neck." All evidence would suggest that this was the original name for the knife, which evolved over time to become "nicker."

The traditional nicker.

123

The third blade
of the Samurai

Japanese civilization has been marked by a series of complex historic events, with quite distinct eras that seethed with wars between the various clans. Soldiers thus constituted a major sector of the population, which was why their weapons received special attention, undergoing constant improvements as the years went by. The first weapon usually mentioned is undoubtedly the sabre. Two thousand years ago this sabre had a straight blade with a single cutting edge, as well as an oval guard and a large hollow pommel: the Kabutsuchi No Tachi. Six hundred years later Chinese influence made itself felt with the appearance of the Chokuto, from which four variants would be developed.

During the Asuka and Nara periods, that is to say until 793 B.C., there was a movement toward great diversity and rich decoration, but it was above all between 794 and 1185 (Heian period) that the most significant development occurred, with the blade becoming progressively curved.

Epochs succeeded each other, with each one standing out due to particular modifications made to the various bladed weapons. In 1876 an edict forbade the carrying of sabres by civilians. Bladesmiths were thus obliged to reconvert, most of the time into tool production. Without the efforts of certain individuals, the ancestral knowledge of these "living national treasures" might well have disappeared forever.

The grading of sabres depends on a multitude of factors, including the type of mounting (jindachi, zukuri, buke sukuri and shira zayal), the period of manufacture (koto, shinto and shin shinto) or even the shape of the blade, as well as its length. If longer than 60 centimeters then it is a daito (tachi and katana); between 30 and 60 centimeters it is a shoto (essentially the short sabre called a wakisashi); shorter than 30 centimeters is a tanto! There is thus no one tanto, but a wide variety, since it is a generic term roughly translated by "dagger." Tantos include the kwaiden, which is a little dagger without a guard that is usually slipped into the folds of a kimono, as well as the aikuchi, more finely worked than the former, or the hamidachi, which has a small tsuba (guard). There is a veritable multitude of other knives in Japanese ancestral tradition,

A tanto may differ according to its era, but is always elegant.

Tsuba.

The sheath is lacquered, as well as being embellished with magnificent decorative symbols.

Certain samurai also practiced archery.

like those slipped into the side of sword sheaths, notably wari bashi, kogai, umabari and kogatana.

Although it is undoubtedly a knife, the tanto belongs to the sabre family, in that it is designed, assembled and placed in a sheath like other swords. It has also undergone the same modifications over the centuries in terms of forging techniques, the shape and design of the blade, and the shape of the point. Initially straight, then curved according to intended use, a tanto blade has always been a fearsome thing, as can be seen from the yoroi doshi, which was an armor piercer, and the "left hand," employed by those who practiced two-sabre combat.

The received idea is that the kissaki, the point of the tanto, must always have that unique beveled profile. In fact, there are a ten-odd different profiles, each one corresponding to a particular use, requirement, epoch or forging tradition. Needless to say they are all listed, graded and coded.

Although it is far from being the everyday knife of all Japanese, the tanto is charged with history and tradition, becoming as legendary as those valiant samurai who carried it with them always.

What a fearsome warrior!

Made in 1980, but according to the strict tradition…

The first Cold Steel model that launched the tanto fashion all over the world.

I n the knife world, it is essential to search continuously for new shapes to please a demanding clientele. Since imagination sometimes runs dry, many have sought their inspiration elsewhere. A traditional knife is often an excellent source from which to work. Various epochs are regularly trawled, as well as foreign countries both near and far. While Japan is a country reputed for its cutlery tradition, it is quite surprising that the original shapes of its blades were totally ignored by Western craftsmen.

This is what led Lynn C. Thompson, an American bladesmith and serious martial arts practitioner, to commence an adventure that led to an explosion of planetary "tantomania" in 1981, for the range of modern tantos that he launched on to the market under the "Cold Steel" brand was an instant success! With a slightly curved blade, beveled point, oval guard as a nod to the tsuba, rubber faceted handle, metal pommel and leather or heat-molded kydex sheath, the resemblance was perfect.

Publicity material related that the quality of the steel and its tempering made this blade indestructible, just like the tantos and katanas of the samurai.

In the United States, Europe and even Japan, retailers were constantly running out of stock for two years running. This tanto vogue did not go unnoticed by other knifemakers, who all set to making their own modern tanto. The most talented were Bob Lunn, Timberline, Doyal Nolen, Bill Pease, Warren Osborne, Phil Hartsfield, Don Fogg, Michael Bell and Don Polizien. The tanto fashion has somewhat eased off now, but the genre is far from being abandoned and some even make it their specialty!

Phil Hartsfield is a great specialist of Japanese models.

For a people who refused to give in

The sheath is always embellished with silver lacework.

Scotland covers 30,000 square miles, divided into Lowlands and Highlands, and is scattered with various clans, from the MacKenzies to the MacGregors and the MacLeods, all with their own particular tartan. Forever coveted by their bellicose English neighbor, an Act of Union merged the two kingdoms, but the conflict was far from over. In 1745 came the Jacobite rebellion, which was put to a bloody end the following year at the battle of Culloden. For the government in London and its various supporters north of the border, the crushing of this rebellion provided the opportunity for a final settling of accounts with the Highlanders, who had been slaughtered in their hundreds, even burned alive!

Scottish power now lay in the hands of those clans loyal to the English Crown, but in order to eliminate any danger from a new rebellion, the Highlanders' spirit had to be crushed.

The traditional dagger of the Highland clans had always been the "dirk." This long triangular blade with a carved handle initially in black bog oak and later on in ebony, was carried in a sheath at the waist, to the right of the *sporran,* a small decorated bag worn on the belt and part of traditional dress.

After the Battle of Culloden, it was forbidden to carry weapons of any kind. But it was too much to expect this proud people with their strong traditions to respect this decree. So the Scots got round this prohibition by hiding a miniature replica of the dirk, the skean dhu, initially in their sleeve, then in their sock. Skean dhu, or *sgian dhu* in Gaelic, means "black knife." The first skean dhu were made from the blades of dirks and claymores (traditional Scottish double-edged sword) that the Highlanders had preferred to break rather than turn them over to the oppressor.

Over time, tempers cooled on both sides and the carrying of the skean dhu became tolerated, then widespread, becoming an integral part of Scottish national dress for civilians and soldiers alike.

The traditional skean dhu.

Ancestral knife of the Inuit

The ulu; the knife of the Inuit.

Migrating north from Asia came many peoples who settled in that vast territory that stretches from Eastern Siberia to the shores of Greenland. The Algonquin tribe of Native Americans called them Eskimos, which means "eaters of raw meat," but their own name for themselves was Inuit, which they proudly translate as "men," inferring "real men" or "supermen!" As the centuries passed, these people developed rites and customs, a particular way of living, clothes that were perfectly suited to the climatic conditions and various objects, including knives of course, whose shape and use varied according to gender.

The ulu, or oulou, is actually a woman's knife for daily use, but which over time came to be used by men also.

The meat that they ate was not cut up on a plate, but carried directly to the mouth and sliced as close as possible to the lips using the blade of the ulu. The half-moon shape of the blade is both practical and symbolic. The symbol is of course that of the moon, of fecundity and of woman…

From a practical point of view, it should be noted that the handle may be firmly grasped even if one is wearing large gloves, and that the shape of the bade is ideal both for scraping a hide before drying it, and then for cutting it. After all, can we not find a very similar tool used by saddlers all over the world to cut leather? The blade was initially made from native copper or else iron from meteorites. The appearance of Russian and European whale hunters enabled the Inuit to barter for good quality steels. As for the handle, it was made essentially from materials originating from animals that the Inuit hunted or fished.

A very old and particularly rudimentary model.

Seductive alternative to the traditional switchblade

The hollow in the miter enables the linear switchblade mechanism to be released using the thumb.

The principle of the primitive knife, that is to say a blade swiveling on an axis to fold into the handle, lasted for a long time: Jambette, Eustache, Capuchin. It can still be found in reproductions, just like the Corsican knife. The inconvenience of such a system is naturally the uncontrolled movement of the blade, since it is held firmly in neither an open nor a closed position. The fitting of a collar on Nontron and Opinel knives, for example, is a safety feature that helps to avoid a major hazard, that of accidentally closing the blade on one's fingers during use. The discovery of the spring was a definite advance, since the blade could no longer swing open in one's pocket. With the Laguiole it was the forced switchblade that was used: the contact parts (blade heel and spring) are fitted in such a way that one has to exert additional pressure on the blade to "force" it to close. The solution was the switchblade, made a specialty by Nogent in its time, with its characteristic ring placed on the back to ensure

its release. The modern switchblade, with a button on the back of the handle, was made popular by Buck in 1963. In 1906, Cattaraugus had patented a linear switchblade system, but it didn't take off. It was only in 1980 that Michael Walker modernized this linear system to produce a real "one-handed" version. The revolution consisted of placing a spring inside the plate, whose extremity would stop against the heel of the blade when open, keeping it firmly in that position. To close the blade the spring just had to be placed against the plate.

By fitting a protuberance on the blade where the thumbnail groove usually was, the blade could be opened and closed easily with the thumb of the hand holding the knife. Opening and closing a knife with just one hand became child's play! The concept of the "liner-lock" and "one-handed" operation was born, and with great success!

Left and right: the liner lock has enabled some surprising shapes.

Many faithful followers even before Rambo

Timberline has proposed some magnificent versions.

Ever since the dawn of time man has been faced with having to survive in the environment in which he finds himself. In an urban setting, where it's certainly not easy every day, the best weapon is surely psychology, but in enemy territory or in an inhospitable environment a little bit more is certainly required. When one mentions the survival knife, one immediately thinks of Sylvester Stallone, whose Rambo films triggered the fashion for this type of knife. But well before 1982, the special forces of all countries were already highly interested in this knife.

During the two World Wars a number of survival-type models had already made their appearance in certain units, whether American, English, Italian or Soviet. Jimmy Lile, a bladesmith in Russellville, Arizona, had already begun to specialize in the genre in 1960. For a long time

Bo Randall had already been selling his n° 14 "Attack" model, which was particularly appreciated by various units in Vietnam: a sturdy 7-inch blade, fitted with a micarta handle with finger-grooves and a strong brass guard with two quillons. But George Ingraham of the 94th Medical Detachment in Vietnam, who was using this model in the line of duty, contacted the Randall workshop to suggest two modifications: adding sawteeth to the spine of the blade and replacing the micarta handle with a hollow metal cylinder closed by a cap on the end, in which various survival accessories could be placed.

This captain in the Medical Corps undoubtedly had serious experience, and his ideas were particularly astute. The parachute cord wrapped around the handle can be used for a variety of purposes. A shaft can be fitted to the hollow handle to make a hunting spear. The sawteeth are most effective for cutting branches and nylon rope. As for the inside of the handle, it can contain water purification or medicinal tablets, as well as accessories for fishing and

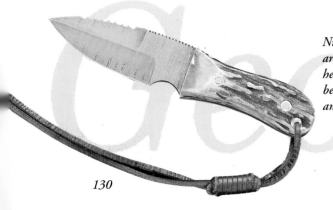

Numerous variants are possible: shown here is a cross between a boot knife and a survival knife.

The most famous survival knife is certainly the one made by Randall.

lighting fires… One can even carry a miniature compass inside, or use the inside of the cap as a reflective mirror for signaling!

The effectiveness of the model was immediately recognized by the various units that adopted it during the Vietnam War. A government-issue model soon followed, intended for Navy pilots. It had been developed by Marble's and was smaller than the Randall version. The survival accessories were contained not in the handle but in a little pack that also included luminous signals, cards, a compass and rations for several days.

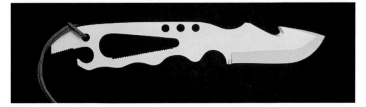

"Skeleton" models offer numerous possibilities.

For the first Rambo film, Sylvester Stallone contacted Jimmy Lile after having heard of his reputation for "survival" models, although Stallone insisted on the "combat" aspect of the knife. Jimmy Lile did a won-derful job, and the attention of the general public was thus caught by a type of knife that had remained rela-tively unknown up until then. For ten years following the release of the film, demand for survival knives was considerable, and once again bladesmiths proved the vital-ity of their imagination. They produced models that were even more imposing than the original, minis-cule ones that were no less effective, and even fold-ing models on which the plaques on the handle had been hollowed out to contain vital accessories.

The best versions of this genre were produced by Timberline, even winning it an award. Survival mania has somewhat died down, like all fashions do, but this is cer-tainly an interesting genre from all points of view and one that is sure to survive!

An amazing invention

The Leatherman range is today vast. This "Wave" is one of the most sought-after models.

itting a folding knife with a blade suited to a variety of professional uses (grafting knife, electrician's knife, etc.) is an old idea, predating even the Swiss Army Knife. So it was but a short step to creating a real toolkit…

But the fundamental difference with the Swiss Army Knife is that the blade is no longer the essential element, but only an accessory. Here the star tool is pair of pliers. This pocket tool set is today manufactured by all of the American knife brands, all rivaling each other for ingenuity. The market is colossal, generating more than 200 million dollars a year. Similar models were produced at the turn of the 20th century though, intended mainly for owners of bicycles.

About twenty-five years ago, the young American Tim Leatherman made a long stay in Europe, during which time he often had to repair the various motor vehicle he used to get around. His "Made In USA" knife was of little use and so he procured himself a Swiss model. Unfortunately this was not that helpful either and he was obliged to buy a set of conventional tools, which were heavy and cumbersome.

Having trained as an engineer, Tim got straight behind his drawing board as soon as he returned to the States, designing the "Leatherman Tool" that would revolutionize the whole world. The tool was just 101 millimeters long, 25 millimeters wide and 11 millimeters thick, for a weight of 146 grams.

This tool set looks like a pair of pliers, with two hollow handles that can contain a multitude of accessories: blade, awl, various screwdrivers, files, can-opener, saw, etc.

Despite its benchmark status, the Leatherman has been much emulated. Today, one can find all shapes and sizes, with more accessories than one could ever imagine.

Al Mar was one of the first to compete with Leatherman.

An unexpected shape for a knife

Mechanism extracted from the handle.

Whether in Norway, Sweden or Finland, the straight knife has long been preferred in Scandinavia to the folding knife. It was not until the middle of the 19th century that a pocket knife was invented, gaining great popularity. This was the "barrel" knife, so called

Used initially in the north of Europe for carving wood, it was soon adopted by sailors and fishermen, before lending itself to all kinds of uses, becoming the all-purpose knife par excellence in this part of the globe. Its inventor produced it in different sizes and even added a corkscrew to it in 1893. In the years that followed, it was sold in France, Great Britain and even the United States, before falling into disuse. Recently, however, it has started coming back into fashion…

because of its characteristic shape. The barrel itself contains the blade, which must be extracted in order to use it.

The barrel knife, with its well-rounded handle.

A metal lug must be pressed to free the mechanism, then the knife pulled out by a ring. The blade itself lies between two brass plates. The blade then swivels out of the plates on its axis, and the ensemble is then slid back into the barrel, which itself now becomes the handle. The reconstituted knife is now as sturdy as any straight model. After use, the procedure is reversed and the barrel can then be slipped back into the pocket from whence it came!

This ingenious system was invented by John Engström in Eskilstuna, Sweden, and patented in 1882.

You just have to press the lug and pull the ring to extract the mechanism.

The barrel knife made over and improved by an inventive cutler

One of the many and magnificent models produced by Alain Descy. A disemboweling hook has been cunningly fitted to this hunting model.

Talented cutlers never limit themselves to reproducing the models in vogue, but ceaselessly seek new shapes and mechanisms so as to innovate and continuously surprise. Among them is Alain Descy, a multitalented man who chose to establish himself in the Drôme Provencale region in the south of France.

His knives are always rather out of the ordinary, whether due to the beauty of their decoration or the ingenuity of their mechanisms.

Intrigued by the barrel knife, Alain Descy turned his full attention to producing a fine hunting knife based on this genre! The blade is of a decent length, available in either forged steel or damascene. The mechanism is that of the original barrel knife, but fitting perfectly without a single millimeter of play. The splendid ebony handle is well rounded and suitably sized to sit well in the hand.

But it was vital that this model stand out from the traditional version. Alain Descy is also a talented artist, and he so he fitted a silver plaque to either side of the handle, onto which he then chiseled some superb animal motifs. And since he himself is also a hunter and thus has a perfect knowledge of the various tasks that have to be undertaken when hunting big game, the heel of the blade, which sticks out of the handle when in the closed position, is fitted with one of a selection of various accessories, like a disemboweling hook, which can be used instantly without having to take out the blade and fix it in place.

But so as to take his inventiveness even further, other models are designed with a totally invisible release catch that is set into one of the miters, which is also chiseled, a nod perhaps to the secret knife…

Continue to surprise us, Mr. Descy, with your talent and your highly individual barrel knives!

Mechanism extracted and blade unfolded.

You have to press the acorn to unlock the mechanism…

Memories of reindeer hunting days…

Traditional Lapp knife (below) with its reindeer antler sheath (above).

Throughout Scandinavia, a region covering the north of Europe that includes Denmark, Finland, Sweden, Norway and Iceland, the climatic conditions are particularly harsh. The northernmost part is inhabited by 40,000 people, the majority of whom live from reindeer herding. They are the Lapps. They are a people with strong traditions, customs, special dress and a guttural language that is similar to the Finno-Ugric languages.

Living in permanent contact with nature, men, women and children are never separated from their traditional knife, the puukko.

Now although the puukko is also the traditional knife of the whole of Scandinavia, the Lapp knife has a number of individual details. Since the reindeer is the basis of their subsistence, the puukko is used to groom them, geld them, brand them, and even slaughter and skin them. Part of the sheath itself is made from reindeer leather, while reindeer antler is used to make the handle, as well as the other part of the sheath. Produced entirely by hand, the blade clearly shows the hammer marks of its forging. Another detail that differentiates the Lapp puukko from its other Scandinavian neighbors is that the pommel completely envelops the tang. The sheath has a characteristic shape, being curved at the bottom, and the entire reindeer antler part is marvelously decorated, either by poker work, engraving or even hemstitch. When the entire sheath is not made in reindeer-antler, the upper part is made from reindeer leather and again decorated. The Lapp puukko exits in various sizes, but is always sumptuous, and the numerous symbols that adorn it remind anyone who might forget that the puukko is much more than just a knife!

The reindeer antler sheath is worked in a multitude of ways; as for the decorations on the leather part, they are all significant.

In the finest Swedish tradition

Characteristic sheath to wear at the belt.

Every country in Europe has its cutlery center: Sheffield for Great Britain; Solingen for Germany; Maniago for Italy, Thiers for France. In Sweden it is Eskilstuna, a town of 90,000 inhabitants near to Lake Mälaren. Prestigious companies have been producing knives here for centuries that have found fame across the country. Some of the oldest firms include Engström, Eka, Segerström and Pontus Holmberg. Since the quality of Swedish steel is well known, their knives have always sold well even beyond their borders. Each brand stands out by its own special models, which are all in the finest Nordic tradition, however.

Pontus Holmberg, founded in 1876 and established in Eskilstuna, has specialized in "outdoor" knives as well as fishing models. Demand for fishing gear is considerable, since Sweden's geographical situation lends itself particularly well to this activity. Pontus Holmberg have concentrated on straight knives that are extremely simple, a one piece blade onto which two plaques are riveted to make a handle. But its particularity is the quality of its steel, its tempering—which gives it an effective and long-lasting cutting-edge—its lightness and the range of blades on offer, since the shape and length of the blade varies according to the work that must be accomplished. Pontus Holmberg have an in-depth knowledge of all the subtleties of fishing that has enabled them to foresee all possible requirements, thus earning them their high reputation. Whether onboard ship or on land, the knife is worn in the belt in a leather sheath that is also in the finest Nordic style.

These models, which were designed at the end of the 19th century, are still produced and just as appreciated today.

Typical shape of the Swedish sailor's knife, produced by Pontus Holmberg.

ROSTFRI

Eight thousand years of history

The belt loop of this is leather sheath is characteristic of Northern Europe, allowing great freedom of movement.

A model produced by the Lisakki company that is typical of the west of Finland, with its horse's head pommel.

Finland is a particularly young country, having obtained its independence by armed struggle only in 1917. This land sits on the Baltic and was initially occupied by the Swedes, then by the Russians, from whom independence literally had to be wrenched, sometimes fighting with just a knife.

It is true that the knife is a strong symbol in Finland. Although "puukko" literally means "knife," it has infinite nuances in Finnish, since it is more than a simple object. Every year in Kauhava in the month of June, there is a show dedicated exclusively to the puukko. The models produced by local craftsmen are still inspired by the shapes of the puukko that was discovered in 1914 and found by carbon-14 dating to be eight thousand years old!

The Finnish puukko generally has a slim blade, a birch handle without a guard, and is worn at the belt in a molded leather sheath. Contrary to the various kinds of sheath that one usually comes across, this one is attached to the belt by a plaited lace, and is flexible, allowing easy movement.

In the west of Finland one also finds another kind of Finnish puukko, of which the model produced by the Lisakki company is quite representative: a brass miter, a handle of layers of leather slices and a brass pommel in the shape of a horse's head, in homage to this animal that has been a faithful companion of man for so long.

Numerous craftsmen, even silversmiths, have reproduced this model, with particularly luxurious finishes. The Marttiini firm has also developed an original range that strictly respects tradition. In order to demonstrate the extent to which the puukko is an integral part of their culture, Finnish designers never miss an opportunity to produce a model according to their own personality. The version produced by the famous stylist Tapio Wirkkala has achieved particular renown.

A typical puukko.

The sharp words of knifemaking

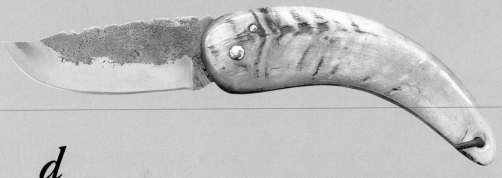

d

DAMASCENE: steel displaying various designs, in the manner of the grain in a plank of wood. These may be in waves, mosaic or other patterns, and are formed according to the way in which steel bars are alternated with others during the forging process.

f

FLAT-SOLE: a straight knife of which the rear section (to which one fixes the handle) is of the same width as the blade.

FORCED SWITCHBLADE: gives a blade a certain rigidity by designing the heel of the blade and the stop in such a way that greater pressure must be exerted to close it than to open it. It is found essentially on the Laguiole.

FULL HANDLE: a straight knife without miters.

g

GRIND: give a knife a cutting-edge using an abrasive method (band; stone).

GUARD (or HILT): generally in metal, this piece is placed between the handle and the blade to ensure safety during use (preventing one's fingers sliding down onto the blade, for example).

GUTTER: hollowed out line running down the blade, either for purely decorative reasons or to lighten the weight of the knife. Originally it was designed for its anti-suction effect.

i

INTEGRAL: refers to a straight knife whose blade, miters, guard and flat-sole are of one piece. To complete the knife one simply fixes two plaques to make the handle.

m

MITER: metal piece fixed to both ends of the handle of a straight or folding knife so as to make these extremities less fragile.

p

PLATES: metal pieces, generally brass, onto which are fixed the handle plaques of a folding knife.

q

QUILLON: The pieces that stick out, generally perpendicular to, the guard, although their shape may well curve up at the end in either direction and be decorated in various ways. The guard may have one or two quillons.

r

RAW FORGED: refers to a blade that has not undergone the usual finishing techniques. Such knives do not have an even, polished appearance, and may even show the hammer marks. These blades are often appreciated for their "rustic" look.

REVERSE-EDGE: part of the point opposite the cutting-edge, but which is

also sharpened. When left blunt, it is called a false reverse-edge.

ROCKWELL: scale measuring the hardness of steel after tempering.

s

SCRIMSHAW: technique consisting of engraving ivory using a fine point; the resulting points and lines are filled with ink to complete the decoration.

SHARPEN: maintain the edge of the blade using an oiled stone with low granular structure and a piece of leather.

SHEATH (or SCABBARD): generally made from leather, this object is designed to hold a straight or folding knife, enabling it to be carried on the belt (occasionally slung around the neck or across the body). They may be decorated in many different ways, including inserts of rare and precious leathers, Indian beading and fringing.

SPINE: Blunt edge of the blade opposite the cutting edge.

STEEL: metal used for knife blades. There exist carbon steels, which are used for forging, and chrome, or stainless steels, that are cut. The two main carbon steels used in France are D2 and XC. There are numerous chrome steels and their quality depends on their composition. The main ones are the 440 (A, B and C), AUS (6, 8 and 10), ATS-34 and Sandvick.

SWITCHBLADE: mechanism designed to enable the blade to be held firmly in the open position; to close the blade one just has to release the lock by depressing a lever or pulling a ring. There also exists the linear switchblade, called "linerlock", which is placed in the line of the internal plate.

t

TANG: fine part extending from the heel of the blade, onto which the handle is fixed.

TEMPERING: essential stage that gives the steel of the blade the best possible metallurgical qualities, without which it would have neither an acceptable cutting-edge, nor durability.

THUMBNAIL GROOVE made either by stamping or scraping out metal on the blade of a folding knife, enabling easier opening of the blade by placing one's thumbnail here.

USEFUL ADRESSES

IMPORTERS:

A.G. RUSSELL
1705 N Thompson St
Springdale, AR 72764-1294
501-751-7341
800-255-9034
501 751-4520
ag@agrussell.com
The oldest knife mail-order company, highest quality. Free catalog available. In these catalogs you will find the newest and the best. If you like knives, this catalog is a must.

ATLANTA CUTLERY CORP.
2143 Gees Mill Rd
Box 839 FD
Conyers, GA 30012
770-922-3700
770-388-0246
www.atlantacutlery.com

BOKER USA, INC.
1550 Balsam ST.
Lakewood, CO 80215-3117
303 462-0662
303 462-0668
bokerusa.worldnet.att.net
www.bokerusa.com
Ceramic blades

C.A.S. IBERIA, INC.
650 INDUstrial Blvd
Sale CREEK, TN 37373
423 332-4700
423 332-7248
cas@casiberia.com
www.casiberia.com
High quality swords, knives and replica weaponry

JOY ENTERPRISES
7516 Central Industrial Dr
Riviera Beach FL 33404
mail@joyenterprises.com
www.joyenterprises.com
Fury™, Mustang™,
Hawg Knives, Muela

KELLAM KNIVES CO.
902 S Dixie Hwy
Lantana FL 33462
561 588-3185
800 390-6918
561 588-3186
info@kellamknives.com
www.kellamknives.com

KOPROMED,
USA
1701 Broadway,
Pmp 282
Vancouver,
WA 98663
360 687-5138
usakopro@aol.com
www.kopromed.com.pl/

**MATTHEWS
CUTLERY**
4401 Sentry Dr.,
Suite K
Tucker, GA 30084

**MESSER
KLÖTZLI**
P.O. Box 104
Hohengasse 3,
CH-3402
Burgdorf, Switzerland
034 422 2378
034 422 7693
info@klotzli.com
www.klotzli.com

PRO CUT
9718 Washburn Rd
Downey, CA 90241
562 803-8778
562 803-8778
procut@earthlink.net
Wholesale only. Full service distributor of domestic & imported quality cutlery. Imports over 200 different models of Toledo made swords from Marto included licensed Hercules & Yena swords.

SWISS ARMY BRANDS INC.
One Research Drive
Shelton, CT 06484
(203) 929-6391
(203) 929-3786
www.swissarmy.com

TAYLOR CUTLERY
P.O. Box 1638
1736 N. Eastman Rd
Kingsport, TN 37662
Smith & Wesson,
John Deere,
Zolan Knives

**UNITED
CUTLERY CORP.**
1425 United Blvd
Sevierville, TN 37876
800-548-0835 orders only
865-428-2532
865-428-2667
order@unitedcutlery.com
www.unitedcutlery.com
Harley-Davidson(tm),
Colt(tm), Stanley(tm)
hunting, camping, fishing, collectible, & fantasy knives

SPORTING CUTLERS:

A.G. RUSSELL
1705 N Thompson St
Springdale, AR 72764-1294
501-751-7341
800-255-9034
501 751-4520
ag@agrussell.com
The oldest knife mail-order company, highest quality. Free catalog available. In these catalogs you will find the newest and the best. If you like knives, this catalog is a must.

AL MAR KNIVES
P.O. Box 2295
Tualatin, OR 97062-2295
503 670-9080
503 639-4789
www.almarknives.com

BEAR MGC CUTLERY
1111 Bear Blvd. SW
Jacksonville, AL 36265
256-435-2227
256-435-9348
Lockback, commemorative, multi tools, high tech & hunting knives

BENCHMADE KNIFE CO. INC.
300 Beaver Creek Rd.
Oregon City, OR 97045
503 655-6004
503 655-6223
info@benchmade.com
www.benchmade.com
Sports, utility, law enforcement, military, gift and semi custom

BERETTA U.S.A. CORP.
17601 Beretta Dr.
Accokeek, MD 20607
301 283-2191
www.berettausa.com
Full range of hunting & specialty knives

BROWNING
One Browning Pl
Morgan, UT 84050
801 876-2711
801 876-3331
www.browning.com
Outdoor hunting & shooting
products

BUCK KNIVES INC.
1900 Weld Blvd.
El Cajon, CA 92020
(800) 735-2825
(800) 733-2825
www.buckknives.com
Sports cutlery

BUSSE COMBAT KNIFE CO.
11651 Co Rd 12
Wauseon, OH 43567
419 923-6471
(419) 923-2337,
busse@bright.net
www.bussecombat.com
Simple & very strong
straight knife designs for
tactical & expedition use

CAMILLUS CUTLERY CO.
54 Main St
Camillus, NY 13031
(315) 672-8111
315-672-8832
www.camillusknives.com
camcut2@aol.com

**CASE, W R & SONS
CUTLERY CO.**
Owens Way
Bradford, PA 16701
800-523-6350
814-368-1736
consumer-relations@wrcase.com
www.wrcase.com
Folding pocket knives

EMERSON KNIVES, INC.
P.O. Box 4180
Torrance CA 90510-4180
310 542-3050
310 793-8730
www.emersonknives.com
Hard use tactical knives; folding
& fixed blades.

GERBER LEGENDARY BLADES
14200 SW 72nd Ave.
Portland, OR 97224
(503) 639-6161
www.gerberblades.com
Knives, multi-tools, axes, saws,
outdoor products

GUTMANN CUTLERY INC.
P.O. Box 2219
Bellingham, WA 98227
(800) 288-5379
www.gutmanncutlery.com,
Jungle knives, Smith & Wesson
Optics, Walther knives and Optics

IMPERIAL SCHRADE CORP.
7 Schrade Ct
Ellenville, NY 12428
800-2-Schrade
800-2-Schrade
www.schradeknives.com

KA-BAR KNIVES INC.
1125 E. State St.
Olean, NY 14760
800 282-0130
www.info@ka-bar.com
<http://www.info@ka-bar.com>

KELLAM KNIVES CO.
902 S Dixie Hwy
Lantana FL 33462
800 390-6918
561 588-3185
561 588-3186
info@kellamknives.com
www.kellamknives.com

Largest selection of Finnish
knives; handmade & production

KERSHAW/KAI CUTLERY CO.
25300 SW Parkway
Wilsonville, OR 97070

KNIVES OF ALASKA, INC.
Charles or Jody
3100 Airport Dr
Denison, TX 75020 8623
903-786-7366
903-786-7371
info@knivesofalaska.com
www.knivesofalaska.com
High quality hunting
& outdoorsmen's knives

**MYERCHIN INC,
GEAR & MARINE CLASSICS**
14185 Regina Dr, Ste G
Rancho Cucamonga CA 91739
(909) 463-6741
(909) 463-6751
myerchin@myerchin.com
www.myerchin.com
Rigging / Police knives

ONTARIO KNIFE COMPANY
26 Empire St
Franklinville, NY 14737
800 222-5233
800 299-2618
salesokc@aol.com
www.ontarioknife.com
Fixed blades, tactical folders,
military & hunting knives,
machetes

**OUTDOOR EDGE CUTLERY
CORP.**
6395 Gunpark Dr, Unit Q
Boulder, CO 80301
303 530-7667
303 530-7020
outdooredge@plinet.com
www.outdooredge.com

**QUEEN CUTLERY
COMPANY**
P.O. Box 500
Franklinville, NY 14737
800 222-5233
800 299-2618
salesokc@aol.com
www.queencutlery.com
Pocket knives, collectibles,
Schatt & Morgan, Robeson,
club knives

**REMINGTON ARMS CO.
INC.**
870 Remington Drive
P.O. Box 700
Madison, NC 27025

**SOG SPECIALTY KNIVES
& TOOLS INC.**
6521 212th St. S.w.
Lynwood, WA 98036
888-SOG-BEST
425 771-7689
sogsales@earthlink.net
www.sogknives.com
ARC-LOCK advantage,
automatic tools

SPYDERCO, INC.
P.O. Box 800
Golden, CO 80402-0800
800 525-7770
303 278-2229
sales@spyderco.com
www.spyderco.com
Knives and sharpeners

TIMBERLINE KNIVES
P.O. Box 600
Getzville, NY 14068-0600
716 877-2200
716 877-2591
gatco@buffnet.net
timberlineknives.com
Precision sharpening
systems

Index

Figures in bold denote pages where the subject is referred to in detail; figures in italics refer to illustrations.

Bibliography

La Coutellerie des origines à nos jours, C. Page, Imprimerie Rivière, 1896-1898

Les Arts du coutelier, J.-J. Perret, 1771

L'Univers des couteaux, J.-N. Mouret, Solar, 1992

Les Couteaux de nos soldats, G. Lecœur et R. Rouquier, Crépin-Leblond, 1998

Histoires de couteaux, guide des collections du musée de la Coutellerie de Thiers, B. Liabeuf, 1995

American magazines
Blade
Tactical Knives
Blade Trade
Knives Illustrated
The National Knife Magazine
Edges

French magazines
Cibles
Excalibur
La Passion des couteaux

Photographic Credits

All photographs are by Gérard Pacella, except for page 9 (bottom) Roger Viollet and page 116 (background) DR.

Acknowledgments

Gérard Pacella, the author, would like to thank all those who gave their precious assistance
to the creation of this book, and in particular:

Brigitte Liabeuf, Curator of the Cutlery Museum in Thiers; Honoré Durand, who graciously welcomed him
to his museum in Laguiole; Mme Kindal and José Martins, who entrusted him with their most beautiful knives;
Christian Moretti and Paulu Biancucci, for their knowledge of Corsican culture;
Ludovic Marsille, for his documentation on Brittany; and of course Sabine and Olivier for their support!

Gérard Pacella, the photographer, would also like to extend his special thanks to Nello Zoppé of Nikon France,
for the loan of the extraordinary PC micro-Nikkor 85mm f/2.8 D
and Zoom micro Nikkor 70-180mm lenses with which all the photographs in this book were taken.

Concept and production by Copyright
Graphic design: Ute-Charlotte Hettler
Layout: Nicole Leymarie
Editorial coordination: Isabelle Raimond
Translation: Roland Glasser